Chasing the
EARLY CHURCH
EXPERIENCE

Katherine Moore Davis, Ed. D.

WESTBOW
PRESS®
A DIVISION OF THOMAS NELSON
& ZONDERVAN

This book is a work of non-fiction. Unless otherwise noted, the author and the publisher make no explicit guarantees as to the accuracy of the information contained in this book and in some cases, names of people and places have been altered to protect their privacy.

WestBow Press books may be ordered through booksellers or by contacting:

WestBow Press
A Division of Thomas Nelson & Zondervan
1663 Liberty Drive
Bloomington, IN 47403
www.westbowpress.com
844-714-3454

Because of the dynamic nature of the Internet, any web addresses or links contained in this book may have changed since publication and may no longer be valid. The views expressed in this work are solely those of the author and do not necessarily reflect the views of the publisher, and the publisher hereby disclaims any responsibility for them.

Any people depicted in stock imagery provided by Getty Images are models, and such images are being used for illustrative purposes only. Certain stock imagery © Getty Images.

Interior Image Credit: unsplash.com

Scripture taken from the King James Version of the Bible.

Scripture taken from The Message. Copyright © 1993, 1994, 1995, 1996, 2000, 2001, 2002. Used by permission of NavPress Publishing Group.

ISBN: 978-1-6642-0810-0 (sc)
ISBN: 978-1-6642-0809-4 (hc)
ISBN: 978-1-6642-0811-7 (e)

Library of Congress Control Number: 2020919375

Print information available on the last page.

WestBow Press rev. date: 10/28/2020

Dedication

To my husband, Victor, who is my gift from God. You are a blessing and the listening ear for me in ministry. Your love, prayers and words of wisdom keep me balanced in my daily walk. I love and appreciate you.

To my beautiful spirit-filled Christian daughters, Charity and Chasity, you have shared me with the world all of your lives. Your love and support of what I stand for and believe in has never wavered. Your sacrifices are appreciated and will be rewarded. I love you so much.

To my precious grand daughter, Kathryn, my name sake. Your innocence, love and wit always captivate my attention. You bring so much joy to my life. With so much love, pride and appreciation, I thank God for you.

To my birth family: My parents, Elmer and Rachel Moore, taught by example. They took us to the House of Worship so we could gain greater insight into our Creator. They instilled Christian values, morals and ethics in all of their children. My parents are in Heaven now, however their fingerprints are forever engraved in the fabric of my memories.

To my siblings, Bobbie, Elmer Jr., Maxine, Tommie and Joanne, who had the same Christian teachings and disciplines that I was afforded. We had fun growing up together, Although Bobbie, Elmer Jr. and Tommie are with the Lord, our family remains strong because we know their address and will see them again. Maxine, your love and support are appreciated.

To my fellow sisters and brothers in the Vineyard: This Ministry was designed for you. God called and anointed me to teach His Word to all people . More than forty glorious years, I have ministered to the Body of Christ as a Fivefold Ministry Teacher. It is with great pleasure that I share with you "For such a time as this".

Contents

Preface

Are you an active participant in a local church fellowship? Are you disappointed in the local church fellowship? Do you see any resemblance of the early church in your local fellowship? Do you witness a family relationship in your local fellowship? Are there miracles of healing and deliverances in your local church fellowship? Is the Word of God {JESUS} taught and actively practiced in the fellowship?

Throughout church history, early teachings that were taught and practiced by the early church and first century believers are unknown. Truths were gradually removed and replaced by popular interests of religious leaders. Today's church exists within tradition and not truth.

Because of my determination to find out why today's church lacks power, I sought the answer from the Word. What was the purpose of the church? What did the early church believe? What did the early church teach? Can power be restored to the church?

Some early church truths have been revived. Justification, Holiness, and Sanctification Doctrines have been restored to the church and is being practiced. Learning how to effectively pray the Word and praying in Tongues are being practiced with success in the church. Believers are using the anointing oil and partaking in the Lord's Supper regularly with numerous benefits. Healing, faith and grace were restored to the church in the twentieth century. It is time to reatore Fivefold Ministry to the church. Fivefold Ministry will strengthen local fellowships with the gifts of five ministerial offices leading and governing the Body of Christ. Single leadership was never apart of Jesus' original plan.

I believe this book will enlighten each reader to what Jesus intended for His church. It is my prayer that this powerful truth will become an eye opener for the believer. We, the church, will only manifest power when we believe and actively practice the teachings of our Founder and Savior, Jesus. This book will teach Jesus' plan and purpose for His church, which has power lying dormant. In this book, we learn to activate the power.

Introduction

My disappointment with the church which is passive concerning the ills of our society led me to research and investigate the problem. This book is a brief summary of my findings and the solution to our present church problem. We were created and designed to please our Creator as written in Revelation 4:11. Racism, poverty, sickness and premature death, etc. are not examples of conditions that please our Creator.

It is not easy to look at ourselves in contrast to God's original plan for our existence. Why? We have to destroy our sacred cows of systemic racism, hatred, gender prejudice, selfishness, ignorance, rebellion, error in teaching and belief, anger and status quo of unfairness, inequality. injustice, etc. We have to voluntarily remove ourselves from the throne of life and eagerly surrender the throne to our Creator. We must believe that God knows all and we know nothing without Holy Spirit revealing the Truth (Jesus) to us. We must sit, listen and learn from those in positions to teach and share biblical truths.

I have been involved in active Christian ministry since age fifteen. For decades I witnessed the most powerful minister in the Protestant church being the pastor. Was this the norm? Yes, according to tradition and error. Why was this one person (at that time a male) so revered and respected as the only voice for God. Knowing that God is not a respector of persons fueled my curiosity and led me on this journey for answers.

Being reared in a Christian home and the church placed me in the company of believers all the time. I was reared to independently think, therefore I startd questioning the status quo. I was faced with the philosophy of those days which said I was female and should accept the male dominance in Christianity. No way, are you kidding? I needed to hear my purpose in life from my Creator. That quest led me to the Word and the origin of biblical teachings and beliefs contrasting many common practices.

It was difficult for me to accept that every ministerial call led to the office of pastor. Approximately fifteen years ago, several pastors began calling themselves bishops. Popularity of the term bishop was dictating the change in semantics. During the last decade, several pastors and bishops are calling themselves apostles. This book is not arguing the popularity of name change. This book supports one ministering in the office that he or she has been called by God. I am seeking the truth from the Word. The intent of this book is to open spiritual eyes that will lead to ministers embracing and walking in their calling with pride and skill of the Word.

When every believer knows and accepts his or her calling, the church will explode with the supernatural and miraculous power that is ours to enjoy daily. The church has been improperly aligned for centuries. This book was written for proper alignment in the church, working together as a unified group of believers in the Body of Christ.

Through my research I am determined more than ever to live the early church life. The fire inside grows stronger each day to receive all the blessings that Jesus gave His life for me to enjoy. I refuse to accept the status quo and a weak, powerless church family. I believe in the early church pattern of divine health and miraculous power. Every second of the day I am seeking others who believe and choose the early church supernatural life. Please join this revolution that empowers the church.

I know that changing the status quo and traditions are difficult. I also know that I have the truth in my argument. The truth is the Word and the Word is Jesus. What did Jesus say on this topic? As you read and study this book, take time to pray and meditate on the message. Allow the Holy Spirit to open your spiritual eyes to His truth which will reveal Jesus' original intent for church leadership. As we learn and begin practicing the early church beliefs daily, we will witness and benefit from the restorative miraculous power active in the church again.

Free Spirit

Who Am I?

*"Thou art worthy, O Lord to receive glory and honor
and power: for thou hast created all things, and
for thy pleasure they are and were created".*

REVELATION 4:11

Born on a plantation in a rural area in the South during segregation witnessing and experiencing unfairness in all areas of life left me questioning my existence. Were some people entitled to better lives because of skin color? Were some people destined to serve others and accept the unfairness and injustices because of skin color? Are some people favored and entitled because of gender?

Reared in a Christian family and never missing a Sunday in a church setting for seventeen years resulted in my asking "Why God why"? The Jesus I saw in the Word accepted ALL people, however I was experiencing toleration instead of acceptance from those professing to be Christians. The answers were not found in conversations. The answers were found in the Bible. God said, "Call unto me, and I will answer thee, and show thee great and mighty things, which thou knowest not". Jeremiah 33:3

I sought my Creator for the answer. God created all of us for His pleasure and I knew God loved me. I also knew God loved all of His creation the same. "Then Peter opened his mouth, and said, Of a truth I perceive that God is no respector of persons". Acts 10:34 God did not create some to experience pleasure and ectasy while others experienced sufferings, pain and disappointments at the hands of others.

Readers, this is where I was decades ago. I needed desperately to understand life and my role in life. Of course I wanted to enjoy the Best Life for me. I wanted to attend school, receive a quality education and give back to society in a positive way. Although segregation was illegal, integration was not being practiced in my rural community. We left the plantation when I was three years old. We moved to town where my parents purchased land and had my childhood home built. I was attending an elementary school with textbooks given to us after the White school across town threw them out. What? When the white school received new textbooks, they sent their old textbooks to us. The binding was worn and torn, some pages missing and marks throughout the books. I wanted to write my name in the book on the page created for the student signature. I was disappointed because that page had been filled six or eight times by others. What? To make it plain, textbooks are outdated when they are published and distributed because history is being made second by second. What did it mean for me at a Black school? My so called new textbooks were at least six years old when I received them. Try explaining to small children why their books are ripped.

My parents were Christians, model citizens, home owners, never arrested, no parking tickets, gainfully employed, paid taxes, attended the local church gathering twice weekly and loved each other. My parents instilled in their six children the love of God, being educated and loving all. What? First, get to know God and accept Jesus as your Savior. I accepted Jesus as my Savior at age eight. I was baptized and became a faithful member of a local congregation of believers.

Second, education is the key to success. In my mother's words, "Go to school, listen and learn". My parents would not accept mediocrity. They preached anybody could be average. Average was the best of the worst or the worst of the best. My parents had not been afforded the best education, however wanted the best for their children. Graduating from high school in a segregated rural community was not designed as the best education. It was enhanced by the zeal of Black educated teachers who taught from books and life experiences that benefited all of us. We were encouraged to think. We asked questions and received answers. Today, students listen to the thoughts of others instead of thinking and questioning the status quo.

Finally integration caught up with my community while I was in high school. What? No white students, just three white teachers. As students, we were not excited because it was evident that they did not want to be there. The rumor mill echoed they were on punishment. Go to the Black school across town or lose your job, I was in each of their classes. Two were kind, however one showed less than toleration and total disrespect to fellow teachers and students. I remember an educator advising me that the local high school in that rural community had its first white student in 2003.

Third, my parents demonstrated love for all, particularly my mother. She would not tolerate negative statements regarding anyone, even when they deserved it. My mother was mulatto, a beautiful fair skinned lady displaying native american cheek bones with straight black hair. Her mother had an ancestral heritage of black, white and native american. Her father's ancestral heritage was white. My grandparents were happily married until his death. I had the pleasure of knowing my maternal grandmother, however my grandfather died before my birth. My mother shared memories with her children referencing his love for his family and work ethic.

During my adolescent years, I was called by God to Pulpit Ministry. What? The denomination I was apart of did not support female ministers. According to them, I could marry a preacher and help him. What about me? To me, this was another form of injustice. I knew this for sure, God knew I was in a female body when He called me. Did God call me to marry a man in ministry to meet his needs, watch him grow in ministry and disregard my calling to ministry? God forbid. "And he gave some, apostles; and some, prophets; and some, evangelists; and some, pastors and teachers. Ephesians 4:11 He was calling me to be a Fivefold Ministry Teacher. I knew I loved education, learning and sharing. I knew I would go to college to be an educator, however this calling was higher than a teacher in the secular world. A secular teacher is a noble profession which I am proud to be a member. A Fivefold Ministry Teacher is a lifetime commitment to the Word (JESUS) and the Body of Christ teaching everyone about His Love for us and His Salvation Package. This Call was ordained to be one of five offices in the Body of Christ to train and equip believers for maturation.

Growing up in the South, attending church gatherings weekly, earning good grades in school, listening to my parents, reading articles and listening to the media say that Black people were created less intelligent resulted in this little black girl investigation. Of course my parents loved their children and were positive while encouraging us to be the best in life. My parents said I was stubborn. Perhaps being stubborn started my quest asking the Lord to provide me with answers. What? I was expected after high school to attend a Historical Black College or University. HBCUs are great, powerful institutions with rich heritages and many notable and professional alums. There were two that most of my teachers had attended and graduated from in my birth state. I was accepted at a large integrated state university. "The effectual fervent prayer of a righteous man availeth much". James 5:16 Through my effective prayers, I received a letter from a school in a neighboring state that I did not apply to and had never heard of its existence. It was a predominately White and Christian private coeducational liberal arts college. Was this my answer? If I apply and I am accepted, I can continue my investigation. I can prove to myself that I can compete successfully. Taking advantage of this opportunity, I began walking and ministering in my created purpose.

I did not share this information with anyone. Looking back, I think I was afraid I would be denied this opportunity. I applied and was accepted. I was given a partial academic scholarship, a grant and work study. This school had about 850 students, appt. 95% White and 5% all other ethnicities. These people were from all over the world speaking several languages. To me, this was a meeting of the United Nations.

I arrived there at age seventeen, a freshmen in a new environment and a new culture. Thinking I would get a Black roommate who was also spreading her wings, I was surprised. Surely, I was not the only lone ranger in the world asking these questions. To my surprise, my new roommate had this white complexion and deep southern accent. I telephoned my parents to summarize the events. In my mother's words, "You are hard headed. You will stay there until the end of the semester and transfer to a HBCU School in the Spring". I was not giving up. My investigation had not been completed. I had no thoughts of leaving. This was the opportunity I prayed for and I was going to see it through. In three weeks, my roommate and I were the best of friends. God used this experience to open my eyes to the truth.

Later, I learned that my roommate was mulatto. Her mother was black and father was white. She had dominant white features. "No weapon that is formed against thee shall prosper; and every tongue that shall rise against thee in judgment thou shalt condemn. This is the heritage of the servants of the LORD, and their righteousness is of me, saith the LORD". Isaiah 54:17 One of the weapons formed against me for seventeen years was Racial and Gender Prejudice. Not only did this weapon not prosper, I had been transformed and delivered from racial injustices. What does this mean? Regardless of the racial disparities, injustices and negative comments spoken and written today, I refuse to return to the feelings and ignorance that I experienced in my early life. I was and am delivered from the hatred and ignorance of others. I have sisters and brothers on this journey with me of all ethnicities who love me as I do them. We appreciate, support and respect each other.

Were there challenges and difficulties? My white college education advisor and professor questioned my presence on campus. He stated that I should have gone to a school for my ethnicity. He attempted to sabotage my growth by unfairly grading my test papers. With the help of a white male student, we overturned his attempts. We traded papers and he graded my paper under the disguise of the other student an A+. He gave the other student's paper under the disguise it was my paper a big in red F. When we approached him, he appeared as a deer caught in the head lights of a speeding vehicle. Knowing that he had been discovered, I moved from hatred to toleration with him.

Decades after graduation until his death whenever in my presence, I always felt his toleration and discomfort. I am very comfortable knowing who I am - a child of the King with a priest and king anointing.

There were white people as well as other ethnicities who viewed me as equal. They were friends and confidantes for me. Some of us are still in contact today. We look forward to the university's homecoming yearly. We have shared retreats and cruises together. Some of my white college friends spend mini vacations at my house. I minister on a regular basis in the university's chapel services. Today the university has a larger percentage of ethnicities on campus, however it is still predominantly white. The central focus of all of us is to love God and His people.

Four years on that campus taught me so much about others as well as myself. I learned to listen and love. The Spirit of Discernment was also being developed in me. I firsthand learned the meaning of the phrase, "By the Grace of God, there goes me". Not everybody had two loving and caring Christian parents in their home. I had witnessed everyday the love and respect my parents shared for each other. Although the denomination I grew up in did not support female ministers, my parents supported my calling. My father was very excited when I was licensed and ordained as a Minister of the Gospel. In my father's words, "If anybody has been called, Katherine has been called by God to preach the Word. She is different and special".

After graduating with a double major in Speech and English Education, I went to work for the federal government as a Secondary School Teacher. I was assigned to an Independent School District with the high school being in decline. What? The students test scores resulted in a loss of state accreditation. More than 70% of the academic staff had been fired and the state lost control of the school. When this happens, the federal government takes temporary control, hires new staff and gives the school a time frame to increase test scores for accreditation. I was interviewed on my college campus after being referred by college personnel. I was hired during the interview to chair the English and Speech Departments. I taught twelfth grade English IV and tenth grade Speech and Drama classes, I had the responsibility of guiding teachers who taught ninth through twelfth grade English and Speech classes. I was the Chairperson of the English Department. Previously this school had all male coaches. Males coached female and male sports. Under this transition, females were sought for coaching positions for female sports. A female coach was verbally hired, however accepted a position before arriving at this school. Since I played college basketball, I was asked to fill in as head basketball coach. The administration ended their search and I became the Girls Head Varsity Basketball and Volleyball Coach for three years.

Serving

Called to Serve

John 13: 34-35."A new commandment I give unto you, That ye love one another; as I have loved you, that ye also love one another. By this shall all men know that ye are my disciples, if ye have love one to another".

JOHN 13: 34-35

I was renting a room from an elderly lady's beautiful four bedroom and two bath home because there were no apartments in this rural community. Her husband was deceased and her sons moved away after college. She never had another female in her house. My presence was a new venture for her.

I was anxious to start my new job. I was a single lady with the skill, lots of time and energy. I was not in a serious relationship and could focus my attention on my calling. I met other new teachers who were very excited about this opportunity. We pledged to turn the negativity of the culture to a positive experience for the school and the community.

We were the first line soldiers for this community. These people did not want to lose their identity by being swallowed up by another school district while abolishing their legacy. They had pride and love for who they had been before this plight. Could we restore them to pride and respect again? We were eager to accept the challenge of constructive change. I was excited remembering the success of Nehemiah in building the wall. "So built we the wall; and all the wall was joined together unto the half thereof: for the people had a mind to work". Nehemiah 4:6

We, the new teachers, had a mind to change the status quo and worked together. It was our focus and commitment to offer the students (black and white) the best education possible. We shared experiences with them to enhance their knowledge beyond the classroom. While teaching Speech and Drama, I took my students to a neighboring city to enjoy their first musical, Old Man River. Although they were teenagers, they were messmerized like a toddler viewing a new tricycle. With the help of the other teachers, the students enjoyed their first parade before football homecoming. The neighboring county allowed their marching high school band's participation. We enjoyed a Junior/Senior Speech Banquet on the lake. The students wore formal attire, enjoyed a great meal, received trophies as the moon cast a shadow on the lake. I saw a transformation of students who had little expectation for their future go through a miraculous methamorphis and dreamed of better lives. It was our priviledge to share love, hopes and dreams with the students so they could experience their best lives. Many of these students have achieved much success and are helping others gain similiar accomplishments.

We appreciated our jobs, our calling and purpose for the season. As new teachers, we were excited to mold the minds of the students as well as the community. We wanted to move the needle from poverty and decline to wealth and upward mobility. I was blessed to have great coworkers in my first professional employment. Although I do not work nor live in that state anymore, I had the pleasure of returning decades later as the High School Commencement Speaker. I was excited to return because the principal extending the invitation was one of my first students. He wore a tuxedo to the Speech Banquet and received a trophy. He attended the O Man River Musical and drove my car in the football parade. For three years I ministered love to that community according to needs - spiritually, academically, athletically, emotionally and socially. Through my behavior hopefully and prayerfully the community viewed me as a disciple of the Lord who loved, respected and appreciated each of them.

During the summer break, I served as a counselor with a federal government program. My assignment was working with disadvantaged teenagers from lower economic homes throughout the state residing on a military base. My Call to Serve manifested in the lives of children suffering from emotional and physical abuse. Thirty years later, I hear from one of the males regularly. He shares his joys, trials and woes from jobs, marriage, alcohol and drug addiction, rehabilitation and families.

I spent more than twenty years working with the adult penal system. My Call to Serve involved Prevention, Treatment, Intervention and Reintegration. What? I was and I am chasing the Believers' Heritage. I am stubborn and determined to live the life that Jesus gave His life for me to enjoy. I want the Early Church Experience of salvations, signs and wonders, miracles and deliverances with Holy Ghost adventures every second of my day. Is this possible or just fantasy? Yes, ALL of this is possible when we believe and practice the teachings of Jesus. "And these signs shall follow them that believe; in my name shall they cast out devils: they shall speak with new tongues: they shall take up serpents; and if they drink any deadly thing, it shall not hurt them: they shall lay hands on the sick and they shall recover." Mark 16:17-18

While working with the adult penal system, I gained knowledge from Judges, District Attorneys, Prosecutors, Police Officers, United States Attorney General's Office, Department of Justice, Probation and Parole Officers, Correctionl Officers, Churches, Ministries, Civic Organizations, Neighborhood Associations, Colleges, Universities, Schools, Politicians, etc. I took pride working with Restorative Justice, ReEntry and Community Corrections Initiatives. It was important to me to involve everyone. I was of the opinion if everyone felt ownership in the pie placed on the table, each would look at their slice with appreciation and gratitude.

My parents had instilled in their children that every person has value even when he or she is unaware of their importance. All of us need to know that someone appreciates, respects and loves us regardless of our present behavior or situations. The investment in another should rise to the extent of wanting to improve him or her without stifling or smothering his or her innate desires. I remind myself often that my Father's most precious creation is His people. I choose to remember how precious we are to Abba Father (our Daddy).

Most of the time when I go to a hospital, I visit the nursery to get a glimpse of the babies (bodies of both gender, different ethnicities, different shapes and sizes totally dependent upon another). I do not see criminals, misfits, degenerates, racists or failures. I see people with the potential to love, create and be positive contributors to society. What happens? Many decades ago, I realized the outcome is determined by who takes the baby home; who teaches and sets examples for the baby; what environment will surround this baby; what opportunities and experiences will be provided for the baby and what character will the people introduced into the life of this baby possess, etc. Before having a child, the mother and father should know the massive responsibility and commitment required for this baby. The parents must know and accept that there is no expiration date to this investment which increases with each generation. When convicted felons stated their problem was the crime which they received a conviction, I said no. I assured them that the conviction was a symptom of a root problem. With the help of Holy Spirit, I discovered the root. When the root was destroyed or eliminated, the symptom (criminal behavior) was never repeated.

There are so many ills in society that can be prevented with knowledge and wisdom of our Creator and His Original Intent for His Creation. Revelation 4:11 reminds us that we were created to please our Father. It pleases our Father for us to be the BEST. What is the BEST? Accepting Jesus Christ as our Savior and receiving His Salvation Package. What is in this Salvation Package? Five Great Gifts-the number of GRACE! The first gift is Salvation (forgiveness of sins). "That if thou shalt confess with thy mouth the Lord Jesus and shalt believe in thine heart that God hath raised him from the dead thou shalt be saved". Romans 10:9 (If you believe in Jesus and His Life, open your mouth and say so). "For whosoever shall call upon the name of the Lord shall be saved". Romans 10:13 (We are whosoevers, and do not need qualifiers). "For I will be merciful to their unrightcousncss, and their sins and their iniquities will I remember no more". Hebrews 8:12 (We have been delivered of past, present and future sins). Because of the Blood of Jesus, our bloodlines were cleansed and we are accepted in the Beloved.

The second gift is Healing (Spiritual, Physical, Emotion, Mental, Psychological, Social and Financial). "Who his own self bare our sins in his own body on the tree, that we, being dead to sins, should live unto righteousness: by whose stripes ye were healed". 1 Peter 2:24 (To be completely well, Abba Daddy provided healing for us in the Body of Jesus; completely well means perfection in ALL areas of our lives).

The third gift is Prosperity (Supernatural Favor and Success in All endeavors). "Beloved, I wish above all things that thou mayest prosper and be in health, even as thy soul prospereth". 3 John 2 (Our Father designed favor and prosperity for each believer so we can assist others in their quest and search for Kingdom living).

The fourth gift is Peace (Serenity, Completion and Wholeness - nothing missing and nothing broken). "Peace I leave with you, my peace I give unto you, not as the world giveth, give I unto you". John 14:27 Jesus was speaking of the aramaic - hebrew word *shalom*. The Brown Driver & Briggs Hebrew Lexicon describes *shalom* as peace, quiet, tranquility, contentment, prosperity, health, welfare, soundness in body, safety, completeness and peace used in human relationships. (Regardless of circumstances and adverse situations each believer should enjoy the Spirit of Peace. Believe and activate peace in our lives daily knowing that *shalom* comes from Jesus).

The fifth gift is Preservation (Security in Salvation). "Father, I will that they also whom thou hast given me, be with me where I am: that they may behold my glory, which thou hast given me: for thou lovedst me before the foundation of the world". John 17:24 (Jesus assures us that we are secure in our salvation. It is His promise that we, as believers, will be with Him. Part of my assignment to the Body of Christ is to go where I am sent by Holy Spirit to serve. I was assigned to a small congregation of white members {who were relatives}. Again, I was the only Black member. I was accepted and loved. I preached and taught the message of Grace. The Pastor was in favor of my preaching and teaching, however it was difficult for the congregation to accept their security in salvation. They were bound by the Law. Each time they had a negative thought or sinned, they would rush to get it under the blood. They believed if they died before getting the sin under the blood, they would go to hell. For years, I preached eternal salvation knowing that Jesus paid our price for salvation on the Cross. Although my assignment changed resulting in a new location, I still love that congregation. I am not sure whether they know today how much Father loves them. It is my prayer that I planted; another watered and the congregation is enjoying the increase today filled with Father's promises). "In hope of eternal life, which God, that cannot lie, promised before the world began"; Titus 1:2 (Daddy CANNOT LIE).

Practicing Convention

The PTIR Model

"The thief cometh not, but for to steal and to kill, and to destroy: I am come that they might have life, and that they might have it more abundantly".

JOHN 10:10

I developed the PTIR Model to assist me in ministry. PTIR is the acronymn for Prevention, Treatment, Intervention and Reintegration. Prevention is the first line of defense. The goal of the Prevention Component is a significant decrease in sinful and negative behaviors, by teaching all people regardless of gender, ethnicity, and beliefs, etc. As Christians, if we use the knowledge and wisdom of Jesus Christ found in Him (The Word) with the assistance of Holy Spirit, we can eliminate or prevent the majority of our mistakes and problems. Through all of my challenges and successes in life, I have asked myself where is the Church? I knew the Church could do more. I knew the Church could do better. Then, I would say the Church is not equipped. As a Fivefold Ministry Teacher, I would seek opportunities to teach and train. I prayed for and asked for opportunities to help all who were interested. These opportunities cost me lots of personal money and time. I remained in secular employment to secure financial funds to provide for my true calling, Moore Life Institute, (my 501 (c) 3 Nonprofit Ministry - a Teaching Resource in the Body of Christ).

Under the direction of Holy Spirit, Moore Life Institute registered with the Internal Revenue Service was created decades ago. I am the Founder, Executive Director and Teaching Facilitator. With the Supernatural Wisdom of Holy Spirit, MLI can develop curricula for solutions to your problems. Call MLI !!! As a member of the church, I want to share with you one of our biggest problems. The church can help decrease this problem as detailed below:

I always remind the Church that we can decrease the number of abortions by teaching and practicing Christian principles. Abortions are the result of sexual intercourse. According to statistics, since 1973 data reported indicated that fifty million abortions have taken place in the United States. This is the number that was reported, therefore more abortions were performed. "Dr. Katherine, how can we decrease the number of abortions"? The Church has to present abortion as a male/female problem equally. Sexual Intercourse resulting in pregnancy is impossible without the involvement of a male and a female. Do you remember in the Bible when the woman was brought before Jesus for punishment by stoning because she was caught in the very act of adultery? (Read John 8: 1-11) Adultery is a sexual act. Although the very act indicated that a man and woman were participating, however the woman was brought without the man. This is a perfect exemple of a double standard.

The Church has to teach that God created sexual intercourse. It was ordained by God for marriage. It is a beautiful, sensous and pleasing act designed for husband and wife. The Church has to provide numerous opportunities for people dating and courting to have fellowship and interaction without engaging and participating in any form of sexual acts. Why do I present it this way? Some people think oral sex would be acceptable behavior for couples and would not result in pregnancy leading to abortion. GOD FORBID!!! Waking up desires involving sexual parts of the body in all forms (heavy petting by fondling, touching, viewing, etc.) is the ENTRY and GATEWAY to sexual intercourse. Dressing in attire that does not show erotic parts of the anatomy should be encouraged for males and females. We can dress appropriately without being half naked. Give each other something to look forward to and enjoy on your honeymoon night.

First, Church, think about it. Sexual Intercourse only in marriage will decrease abortions by a large number. The result would be children entering this world with a mother and father residing in the same home and committed to being Godly examples.

Second, bible teaching and practicing Christian principles by being our brother's keeper would decrease abortions. Changing the mind and thoughts of people regarding sexual intercourse would decrease the number of rapes and molestations.

Third, Church providing proper teaching to spouses would prevent couples from being involved in sexual intercourse when it is unwanted and resulting in pregnancy, which leads to abortion. Spouses, learn to effectively enjoy this gift God gave you.

Fourth, Christians do not shame an unmarried pregnant female. Remember the guilty male maybe sitting among you. The male is equally responsible for this pregnancy. Encourage and love her. If she chooses to mother her child, assist her and encourage the father to render emotional and financial support. If she does not want to mother this child, steer her toward adoption. There are many barren couples and fertile couples wanting to increase their family size.

Whether abortion is legal or illegal; it will always be present. We can decrease the number of abortions significantly by educating our people and practicing what we are taught from the Bible. Church, lets be doers and not hearers only. (James 1:22)

I created in the PTIR Model, when it is too late to benefit from the Prevention Phase, the Treatment Component. In the Treatment Phase, believers are taught how to practice Christian lifestyles by following the principles and teachings of Jesus Christ. Come on CHURCH, lets work together to celebrate Christian lifestyles. To best accomplish this task, small groups, life groups and cell groups addressing issues are sought for attendance. (Alcoholic Anonymous, Narcotics Anonymous and Gamblers Anonymous are very successful assisting those with alcohol, drug and gambling addictions). The church works with grief, divorce, eating disorders and other issues without attendees feeling guilty, nervous or embarassed.

I had the pleasure of working with citizens who were interested in improving the image of their town. While visiting and researching the history of the town, I was of the opinion that a major cosmetic makeover would be the focus. I needed to gain partners in this endeavor. I met with town officials several times. Each meeting, the group increased in numbers, thereby granting me the partners I needed for this ultimate task. The partners were: Mayor, City Councilpersons, Chief of Police, Sheriff and Deputies, Fire Chief, 4-H, Prison Wardens, Educators, Business Owners, Probation & Parole Officers, Sanitation Dept., Parks and Recreation, Volunteers, Probationers, Parolees, etc. This town had two major U.S. Highways intersecting in this locale. I chose to focus on the cosmetic makeup of the two roadways which were entrances to the town north/south and east/west.

The cosmetic makeover was scheduled for a Saturday in the spring of the year. We gathered with the attitude of Nehemiah. We had a mind to work as recorded in the fourth chapter and six verse of Neremiah. I was very interested because this was my homeland, just as Nehemiah. It was cold that morning. All were eager to do their part. The citizens wore their civic pride and the probationers and parolees completed community service work. We picked up trash, litter, debris and garbage. We mowed and raked grass. We planted flowers. Having 4-H as a partner afforded the opportunity of knowledge of the best flowers and plants for the area. 4-H donated the flowers, plant and shrubs. We weedeated and trimmed sidewalks. The Sanitation Dept. brought several mowers, weedeaters, hedge trimmers and power saws. We bagged clippings, trimmed and pruned limbs. The bagged items were loaded on the dump trucks. At the end of the day, we gathered at the Community Center. I expressed my appreciation and gratitude for each person, gave each organization a certificate and assigned a mile section of the roadways to different partners to maintain. Months later, they expressed their competitive nature by stating that they passed their assigned section daily and would stop to pick up any litter or trash. This event labeled as Treatment for a physically weak and infirmed town resulted in a beautiful cosmetic makeover. Although this was approximately fifteen years ago, I travel through this town several times a year always smiling and remembering the collaborative effort of male/female and black/white working side by side on a cold day.

The third phase of the PTIR Model is Intervention. When we are beyond the Prevention and Treatment Phases, we are ripe for an Intervention, (Tough Love). The goal of Intervention in the Church is assisting backsliders, ignorant and uninformed people through innovative methods of introducing Christian principles in everyday practices and lifestyles. Sometimes confinement, inpatient and incarceration tactics are the result. We, the Church must be eager and willing to demonstrate Tough Love. No excuses and no regrets to help a sister or brother in need. Paul instructed the Corinthian Church to withdraw fellowship from a brother that was practicing sexual immorality in the fifth chapter of 1 Corinthians. Paul stated "Therefore put away from among yourselves that wicked person." {1 Corinthians 5:13

An example of Intervention in action was a teenage white male who thought it was funny to destroy mailboxes. He would drive through neighborhoods plowing and mowing down mailboxes for entertainment. He was finally arrested and charged with a misdemeanor referencing to several counts of destruction of property. In the punitive phase, an elderly woman stated that she received her prescribed medication through the mail. Because her mailbox had been destroyed, the letter carrier could not deliver the prescribed medication. It is against postal guidelines to leave mail without a receptacle that meets federal regulations. This lady stated that she did not have any medication and was without refills for almost a week. She had to purchase a mail receptacle and hire someone to properly place it on the street in front of her house. The guilty young man was sentenced to six months of community service assisting elderly people in retirement and nursing homes. He spent time reading, listening and helping elderly people eight to ten hours weekly. At the end of his community service, the young man continued visiting the centers for a few hours on Saturdays.

The fourth phase of the PTIR Model is Reintegration. After

Intervention has taken place and the punitive phase is complete, what is the next step? We must introduce him or her back into society through Reintegration. The goal is to walk with the believer for a period of time. (The believer, similiar to a hospital patient, has been released from the hospital; but is still recovering and not fully restored. The transition is monitored with medical advice). In II Corinthians 2, Paul instructed the Corinthian Church to restore the brother who had received the hand of fellowship withdrawal in 1 Corinthian 5. Paul instructed the Galatian Church in spiritual restoration in Galatians 6:1 "Brethren, if a man be overtaken in a fault, ye which are spiritual, restore such an one in the spirit of meekness; considering thyself, lest thou also be tempted". Church, lets practice restoration with gentleness and empathy without judgment, remembering that we can be tempted and fail.

An example of the PTIR Model in action was a black adult male who lived in a rural community. Most of the employers were white and this young man was convinced that he was denied employment due to his ethnicity and felony conviction. I was addressing scores of black, white, male and female adult felons on probation and parole in that rural community. It was a beautiful, warm and sunny Friday. I drove approximately 325 miles monthly to face to face visit my partners and address the convicted felons in that community. My intent was to prove that my baby, PTIR, was efficient in whatever stage an individual found him/herself. I had employers who served as partners with me in that area. These partners were law enforcement, ministers, educators, treatment counselors, employers, politicians, community leaders, etc.

While speaking with words of motivation to stimulate the listeners, this young man said with a doubtful and angry voice, "Dr. Katherine, maybe what you say works in your city, but not here. Nobody will give us a job here. I been to prison and I am black. Can you fix that"? Determined to prevent a discourse of anger and argumentation, I asked him to remain after I completed my work with the group. I was confident that I could help. Why? Holy Spirit lives inside of me and knows everything.

After the group left the building, I allowed the young man to rehearse his complaint again. This young man was in Phase Four, Reintegration. He had been convicted of a crime; sentenced to prison; paroled to his hometown; but lack of employment. I asked him a question, What is my race? The young black male said, "You are black". I asked him had he applied for jobs. He said, "lots of time". The largest employer in that area was a catfish farm. Private individuals and businesses spent tens of thousand dollars annually purchasing catfish in bulk. The employers needed workers and were not concerned about race (ethnicity). gender or criminal records. This company was operating a business, not an organizaton emphasizing racial divide and disparities.

It was my opportunity to speak boldly or as we, Southerners, say "where the tire meets the road". I shared with him, although we were the same ethnicity, I would not hire him. My rejection did not have anything to do with his felony conviction. If I was hiring for a business, his appearance would be my number one concern. I would have to make sure that the majority of my customers were not intimidated by my employees. His hair was not combed and had not been combed for a long time. He was wearing pants several sizes too large. He said each time he applied for work, he wore clothes similar to what he wore that day. I suggested that he comb his hair and purchase clothing that fit. I was confident that he would have a better outcome if he presented himself as one desiring a job. The young man was quiet, but did not believe me. He left saying, "These white people just hate us". I left there praying in my car knowing that Father God had a job for him. I wanted him to destroy his root of unemployment. He needed to change his physical appearance and employment would manifest.

The following month, I returned to this same community. I was speaking to a group of convicted felons. Before I departed while gathering my paraphenalia and in the room alone, an adult black male approached me. Not aware of who he was, but extending personal amenities with hello and a smile, he began to speak. He asked, "Do you remember me". I answered no. I addressed hundreds of people daily of both gender and several ethnicities. Unless someone drew my attention because of an interaction, etc. seldom I remembered random individuals. I rarely addressed the same audience.

He was determined to refresh my memory. He advised me that he was the young man that I took time to speak to one on one the month before about his lack of employment. I recalled the incident, however his appearance had changed drastically. He shared with me that he was angry with me last month because I did not understand. He was determined to prove me wrong and left the meeting on a mission. He went to a local barbershop and received a short hair cut. He went to a local store called Super Ten and purchased a pair of blue jeans for $10. It was 1:00 p.m. on a Friday afternoon, but determined to prove me wrong, he went to the Catfish Farm Employer. He completed the application; was interviewed; was hired and went to work about 2:00 p.m. that same day.

I asked. "Can you sit with me a few minutes"? He agreed and had a hour before his shift. I expressed how excited I was about his employment, but more excited because this man's beliefs changed. He was of the opinion that the employer was racist. I asked him whether the company had changed owners. I wanted to know if the owners or management was black. He laughed heartily stating the same man talked to him each time he came. I asked him whether he understood the difference between business and personal issues now. Once again laughing and nodding, he assured me that he would never be judged again by a slouching and unkempt appearance.

Through my baby, PTIR Model Phase Four - Reintegration, this young man's opinion that he thought was factual about white and black people was torn down. He believed that all white people were racially prejudiced and hated all black people. He found out in a few hours on one Friday after listening to me; determined to prove me wrong that he could be gainfully employed by presenting himself as an employable risk. I believe this young man helped change similiar opinions of others because of his attitude adjustment gained from the above experience.

We Are Our Brothers' Keeper

Is There A Cause?

---

*"And Eliab, his eldest brother heard when he spake unto the men;
and Eliab's anger was kindled against David, and he said, Why
camest thou down here? and with whomest has thou left those few
sheep in the wilderness? I know thy pride and the naughtiness of
thine heart; for thou art come down that thou mightest see the battle.
And David said, What have I now done? Is there not a cause?"*

I SAMUEL 17: 28-29

D r. Katherine, why are you shaking things up and asking questions? When Eliab did not have the answer and resented his brother's presence, David remarked is there not a reason for me to be concerned. I have the concern of the status of the Church. We are declining in church attendance, church membership and <u>Power</u> in the Church. Less individuals are attending and visiting weekly places of worship where the Church gathers to commune and fellowship. Less people are uniting and becoming apart of local fellowships who call themselves Christians. There are less testimonies of people witnessing and receiving the manifested power of God's presence in the local Church.

If I can shake up the Body of Christ and move us to action, then I shout "Hallelujah". Our Father in Heaven (my Daddy) gave HIS BEST, JESUS, to us. We are the Church called out of this world to represent Jesus Christ on earth. Lets put things back in order and show this world that the Head of the Church (JESUS) is still leading us. Jesus represents love, acceptance and unity.

What is my concern? The Church was given power however it is not evident in our everyday lives. "And these signs shall follow them that believe, In my name shall they cast out devils: they shall speak with new tongues; They shall take up serpents, and if they drink any deadly thing: it shall not hurt them; they shall lay hands on the sick, and they shall recover." Mark 16:17-18 Most Christians do not believe in the above, therefore do not practice the above verses. These Christians live defeated lives and are dying in weak and ill congregations. Yes, this is a bold statement, however I was an active member of this group for decades. Had I prematurely died, I would have gone to Heaven without experiencing the rich heritage that Jesus secured for me and every believer on the Cross. I am the Righteousness of God in Jesus Christ because of His finished work on the Cross.

If you (the reader) are not convinced of the need for the Early Church Experience by now, continue with me as I present my plight to believers. This year is 2020 and I am extremely disappointed with Today's Church settling for the status quo of the mediocre manifestations (at best). What? Sickness, anger, racial prejudice, gender disrespect, sexual molestation, ignorance of Christian principles, poverty, illicit alcohol and drug usage, decrease in moral values, teaching errors and beliefs about the Word, profane speech, etc. are a few of the behaviors witnessed each day which contribute to moral decline of society. Today's church is demonstrating spiritual blindness and toleration. Jesus came to the earth, demonstrated the Christian lifestyle, gave ALL (HIS LIFE) by dying for everybody, resurrecting from the dead and sitting at the right hand of our Father for one reason - THE ABSOLUTE BEST FOR ALL OF US!!!

As I chase the Early Church experience, I am reminded of preparation and training the church offered as well as received before commission for service. The original apostles spent three years with Jesus. They sat at the feet of Jesus, being taught by their Creator. They witnessed Jesus' behavior manifesting in love, compassion, respect, healings, signs and wonders, miracles, deliverances, salvations and dead bodies raised to life, etc. After experiencing the blessed life, how does one return to a weak, sick, defeated existence? They can and will not settle for a mediocre existence any longer. The early church taught and practiced the examples of Jesus.

The church at Antioch was a multicutural congregation being guided by Holy Spirit. "Now there were in the church that was at Antioch certain prophets and teachers; as Barnabas, and Simeon that was called Niger and Lucius of Cyrene, and Manaen, which had been brought up with Herod the tetrarch, amd Saul. As they ministered to the Lord, and fasted, the Holy Ghost said, Separate me Barnabas and Saul for the work whereunto I have called them. And when they had fasted and prayed, and laid their hands on them, they sent them away. So they, being sent forth by the Holy Ghost..." {Acts 13: 1-4} There were African and Asian leaders denoted in their names and origin of birth. As Acts 13:1 stated two of the fivefold minister offices {prophet and teacher} were directed by Holy Spirit to lay hands and separate Barnabas and Saul, whose name was changed to Paul, to the work of the ministry.

For decades, I have been apart of congregations that welcome people of different ethnicities. I am chasing the appreciation of each believer's gift regardless of gender and ethnicity mirroring the early church fellowships . In the early church, Phoebe and Priscilla (women) were respected ministers and co laborers with Paul as stated in Romans 16: 1-4. "When every believer, regardless of gender and ethnicity, is loved and respected for his/her spiritual calling and natural ability to do the work of the ministry guided by Holy Spirit, I am living the Best of Life.

Take a moment and ask yourself, am I experiencing the BEST OF LIFE? If not, take several minutes pondering the difference and the problem. Think of what you desire for your life, family, friends and the world. JESUS is our GRACE. He loved us so much that he sacrificed EVERYTHING for all. Lets decide to show our appreciation for His Gift of Jesus by believing, receiving, activating and applying the Salvation Package in our daily lives. Thank you Daddy for ALL - You, Jesus and Holy Spirit! As Christians, we should strive to live the life Jesus died for us to enjoy.

Dr. Katherine, I am answering the question. No, I am not living the best life. As a matter of fact, I am disappointed and depressed. What can I do? You must desire and refuse to accept NOTHING LESS THAN the Early Church Experience. Lets explore the supernatural and miraculous formula of the Early Church. Lets go to the book of Acts. This is the history of the Early Church believers: their purpose, beliefs, acts, supernatural and miraculous successes manifesting in everyday lives.

The Early Church had the WORD, Prayer (Praying in Tongues), Praise & Worship, Divine Healing, Anointing Oil, Lord's Supper and Fivefold Ministry. Do we still have the above? Yes, it has not gone away. IT IS LYING DORMANT. Church, join me in waking these GIFTS. "Father, forgive us for not using our Weapons of Victory. We welcome the Anointed and Holy Ghost Arsenal back to the church in Jesus Name."

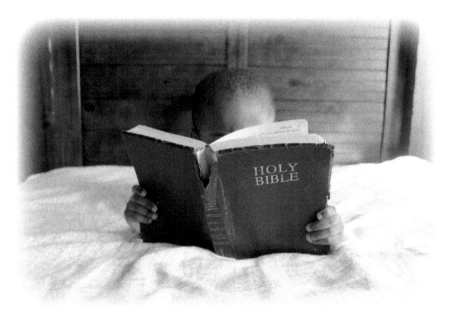

Jesus is the Word

The Word (Jesus)

"In the beginning was the Word, and the Word was with God, and the Word was God". John 1:1 "And the Word was made flesh and dwelt among us, (and we beheld his glory, the glory as of the only begotten of the Father,) full of grace and truth."

JOHN 1:14

Jesus is the Head of the Church as stated in Colossians 1:18. "And he is the head of the body, the church: who is the beginning, the firstborn from the dead: that in all *things* he might have the pre-eminence." Jesus has supremacy in all things. Jesus has first place in all things. Life from nothing began through him, and life from the dead began through him, and he is, therefore, justly called the Lord of all as stated in the J. B. Phillips New Testament. The Message Bible describes the Head of the Church; "He was supreme in the beginning and - leading the resurrection parade - he is supreme in the end. From beginning to ending he's there, towering far above everything, everyone."

"He saith unto them, but whom say ye that I am? And Simon Peter answered and said, Thou art the Christ, the Son of the living God. And Jesus answered and said unto him, Blessed art thou, Simon Barjona: for flesh and blood hath not revealed it unto thee, but my Father which is in heaven, And I say also unto thee, That thou art Peter and upon this rock I will build my church; and the gates of hell shall not prevail against it. And I will give unto thee the keys of the kingdom of heaven: and whatsoever thou shalt bind on earth shall be bound in heaven: and whatsoever thou shalt loose on earth shall be loosed in heaven." Matthew 16: 15-19 After God revealed to Peter the identity of His Son, Jesus the Christ; Jesus revealed to Peter his true identity. Jesus called Peter a Rock and stated that all those who confessed Him (Jesus) as God's Son would become the Church.

The Church is a large living organism that can not be defeated. The Church can do all things through Christ who strengthens us as stated in Philippians 4:13. Because of Jesus Christ, The Anointed One and His Anointing, we can do all supernatural and natural things. There are no impossibilities in Jesus Christ for the Church. "For the word of God is quick, and powerful, and sharper that any twoedged sword, piercing even to the dividing asunder of soul and spirit, and of the joints and marrow, and is a discerner of the thoughts and intents of the heart." Hebrews 4:12

The Word of God was ALIVE in and to the Early Church. Inside of the Early Church, bodies were lively with great anticipation and expectation that resulted in supernatural manifestations. The Early Church had great faith in the Word (Jesus). They spoke the TRUTH (Jesus) and saw what they spoke, which attracted naysayers and others to this movement - the GOSPEL (Good News).

The Word of God has to be resuscitated in today's church. Many believers have the knowledge of the Word of God on life support. The Word of God will never die, but is dormant in the lives of many believers. We must read and meditate upon the Good News with passionate hearts. Allow Holy Spirit to open our hearts to the Word of God. Do you remember when Jesus shared the role of Holy Spirit with his disciples? "Howbeit when he, the Spirit of truth, is come, he will guide you into all truth: for he shall not speak of himself; but whatsoever he shall hear, that shall he speak: and he will show you things to come. He shall glorify me: for he shall receive of mine, and shall show it unto you." John 16: 13-14 What was Jesus saying? Jesus was reassuring us that we would not have to create a plan; would not have to question what he desired for us and would not wonder whether we had the correct interpretation of Jesus.

God, Who is Omniscient (All Knowing), has provided these answers without our input. Before we believe that we can not understand the Word of God; God provided the answers with the Greatest Teacher in the Person of Holy Spirit. Ask Holy Spirit, Who has ALL the answers. Holy Spirit knows everything about the Word of God (Jesus). His mission is to teach us. Church, lets sit at his feet in the Word; turn off our natural minds and receive the deepest and richest knowledge of Jesus. The Early Church believed the Word; was taught by Holy Spirit and put that PERFECT WISDOM into action in their daily lives. Salvations, healings, signs/wonders, deliverances and miracles manifested daily with the Power of Holy Spirit guiding the Early Church.

Believers are more than conquerors as stated in Romans 8:37. Jesus gave the Church the victory as stated in 1 Corinthians 15:57. Jesus always causes the Church to triumph, so why are we living in defeat? Perhaps we are not adhering to the principles and standards that Jesus set forth for HIS CHURCH.

The Early Church knew Jesus and wanted to embrace His teachings. Many of them, particularly, the original Apostles had personal knowledge of Jesus. They walked with Him, witnessed His ministry; ordained and called to ministry by Him and repeated His actions with new followers. The disciples knew Jesus was crucified and witnessed his resurrection. They spent time with him after his resurrection. They were present at Mount Olive when he ascended to heaven. They listened to his instructions and gathered as a unified group in the Upper Room to wait for the Promise, Holy Spirit. On the tenth day after Jesus' Ascension, Power came to the Church. "And when the day of Pentecost was fully come, they were all with one accord in one place. And suddenly there came a sound from heaven as of a rushing mighty wind, and it filled all the house where they were sitting. And there appeared unto them cloven tongues like as of fire, and it sat upon each of them. And they were all filled with the Holy Ghost, and began to speak with other tongues, as the Spirit gave them utterance." Acts 2: 1-4

The Early Church did not attempt to start a new ministry. They knew Christianity was the only way. “And the disciples were first called Christians in Antioch.” Acts 11:26 They practiced and patterned the teachings of Jesus to the consistency of non believers mocking and calling them “little Christs”. The results were phenomenal which increased the growth of the Early Church. “And the Lord added to the church daily such as should be saved.” Acts 2:47

The Early Church knew the difference between Christianity and Judaism. The new converts did not attempt to add Judaism to their beliefs in Christianity. They did not mix the Law that was the central focus of Judaism with Grace, the teachings of Jesus Christ. The Early Church in Galatia was admonished by Apostle Paul in Galatians 3:1. “O foolish Galatians, who hath bewitched you, that ye should not obey the truth, before whose eyes Jesus Christ hath been evidently set forth, cricified among you?” Apostle Paul said. “Stand fast therefore in the liberty wherewith Christ hath made us free, and be not entangled again with the yoke of bondage.” Galatians 5:1 Apostle Paul could speak and write on this subject because he was steeped in the law which blinded him to the Truth (JESUS) until his Damascus Road experience. Paul had been the Chief Persecutor of the Church. At the time of his writings and teachings he had become the Apostolic Voice for the Early Church teaching Grace and only Grace. Grace is the Person Jesus and does not need a qualifier or additive. Thank God for Grace (Jesus).

“Study to show thyself approved; a workman needeth not to be ashamed rightly dividing the word of truth.” 2 Timothy 2:15 If we do not study Jesus and allow him to become an integral part of our very being, we will be ineffective and unsuccessful in our Christian walk. An operative word in the above verse is rightly meaning we can wrongly divide the truth. “These were more noble than those in Thessalonica, in that they received the word with all readiness of mind, and searched the scriptures daily, whether these things were so.” Acts 17:11 As a fivefold minister teacher, I have so much respect for the Bereans. Why? The Bereans did not receive the words of preachers to be true without searching the scriptures daily for validity. The Berean Jews did not demonstrate petty and mean characteristics as the Thessalonian Jews.

"So then faith cometh by hearing, and hearing by the word of God." Romans 10:17 Our faith increases as we hear repetitively the words of Jesus (the Rhema Word). Since Jesus is the Founder of the Church, Author and Finisher of our faith, we should listen and follow his teachings. As a member of the Body of Christ, we gladly adhere to the Word of God (Jesus). We store the Word of God in our hearts with meditation, so we will not sin against God. Psalm 119:11 Every Word of God is true. Proverbs 30:5 In Luke 11:28, we are blessed when we hear and practice the Word of God. Jesus reminds us that he is our Sanctifier and our Truth in John 17:17. There is no expiration date on the Word of God. The grass withers and flowers fade, however the Word of God stands forever. Isaiah 40:8 Laws change and amendments are added to legislation, however the Word of God is true and everlasting. The words of God stand forever. 1 Peter 1:25 O Lord, your word is firmly fixed in the heavens written in Psalm 119:18 What a comfort and peace we eternally inherit as christians knowing that heaven and earth will pass away, but never the words of Jesus in Matthew 34:25. Looking for encouragement, read Psalm 12:6, the words of God are pure words. As believers, we have tasted the goodness of the Word of God. Hebrews 6:5

The Early Church read, believed, shared, taught and practiced the Word of God daily. The Word of God was used as a dietary supplement for daily nourishment. They were faithful to the teachings of Jesus. "The Book of the Law shall not depart from your mouth, but you shall meditate on it day and night, so you may be careful to do according to all that is written in it. For then you will make your way prosperous, and then you will have good success." Joshua 1: 8-9

The Early Church believed the Word. They practiced the Word. They asked for boldness to teach others, with little or no thought of sufferings to themselves. They experienced beatings, imprisonments, exile and premature death and continued teaching and preaching the Word of God (Jesus). "Therefore let all the house of Israel know assuredly, that God hath made that same Jesus, whom ye have crucified, both Lord and Christ." Acts 2:36 What was the result of Peter's message? "Then they that gladly received his word were baptized; and the same day there were added unto them about three thousand souls." Acts 2:41

As we study the Word of God with Holy Spirit, we will supernaturally experience the intimate love of our Heavenly Father. Our time in the Word heals, renews, restores and tansforms us. Our Father loved mankind so much that He gave His only begotten Son, Jesus, to die on the cross to save and ransom us. "For God so loved the world that He gave His only begotten Son, that whoever believes in Him should not perish but have everlating life." John 3:16

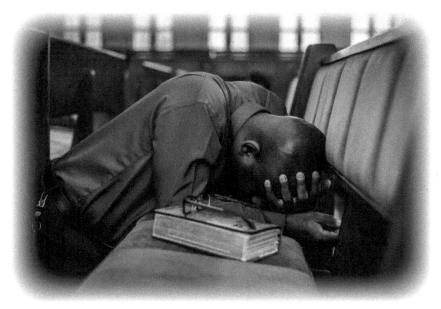

Communicating with my Father

The Power of Prayer

"And it came to pass in those days, that he went out into a mountain to pray, and continued all night in prayer to God."

LUKE 6:12

Prayer is intimate fellowship with our Father. Prayer allows us the opportunity to commune with the Father and allow Him time to commune (speak) to us. Prayer is asking and receiving, seeking and finding and knocking and opening. Matthew 17: 7-11 When we ask our Father according to his Word, we receive His promises. When we seek our Father, we find Him. He is always present to us. When we knock on His heart, He opens the door for us to come in and fellowship with Him.

Prayer is a powerful weapon available to everybody. Dr. Katherine, why do you think prayer has power? Jesus, the Head of the Church prayed often. In Luke 6:12, Jesus spent all night in prayer. What was Jesus doing? He was spending intimate and personal time with Father God. He was in fellowship with the Creator - Abba Father. Jesus was about to make a very important decision. He was going to choose twelve people from his large group of disciples. The twelve were called Apostles and became the Early Church leaders. They would embark upon three years of the Greatest Internship under the training, leadership, guidance and direction of Jesus Christ, The Anointed One and His Anointing, Who removed all burdens and destroyed all yokes.

"The effectual fervent prayer of a righteous man availeth much." James 5:16 If we know who we are praying to; know how to pray and what we are praying about, we will have victory. The earnest (heartfelt continued) prayer of a righteous man makes tremendous power available (dynamic in its working)." James, the half-brother of Jesus is the author of this book in the Bible. He has been described by many historians and bible scholars as the "Callus Knee" preacher. He spent many hours on his knees in prayer. He was the righteous man who prayed earnestly and effectively while reaping the results. James 5:16 (Amplified Classic) Have you ever thought about the dynamic power that is available to us when we choose to talk to our Father in Heaven? We have access to the MOST POWERFUL DEITY that has or will ever exist? Father God gave us access to Him as Jesus was paying the price for our access on the Cross.

"And thou shalt make a veil of blue, and purple, and scarlet, and fine twined linen of cunning work: with cherubims shall it be made: And thou shalt hang it upon four pillars of shittim wood overlaid with gold: their hooks shall be of gold, upon the four sockets of silver. And thou shalt hang up the veil under the taches, that thou mayest bring in thither within the veil the ark of the testimony: and the veil shall divide unto you between the holy place and the most holy." Exodus 26: 31-33

God had given Moses specific instructions in constructing the veil in the tabernacle. The veil was the divider and separator between the Most Holy One and the Holy Place. It was sturdy and strong, built to last. The Jewish historian, Josephus, described the veil as 60 ft. x 60 ft, with gold thread woven through. Josephus said a team of horses could not pull down or tear the veil apart. God's glory was kept inside of the Holy Place. High priests were the only people allowed into the Holy Place once a year to offer sacrifices. "And the LORD said unto Moses, Speak unto Aaron thy brother, that he come not at all times unto the holy place within the veil before the mercy seat, which is upon the ark; that he die not: for I will appear in the cloud upon the mercy seat." Leviticus 16:2

"And Jesus cried with a loud voice, and gave up the ghost. And the veil of the temple was rent in twain from the top to the bottom."

Mark 15: 37-38 Before this act, the veil separated God and mankind. God's glory was hidden from us because the glory would destroy us because of our sin. Jesus exchanged His Righteousness for our sins on the Cross. When the exchange was complete, Jesus said "It is finished". John 19:30. No man could reach the top of the veil or anticipated this miraculous event on Golgotha, the Place of the Skull, Calvary, (the Cross). Who tore the veil? Father God Himself tore the veil and allowed His family freedom and unrestricted access to Him anytime that we desire to speak with Him. Thank you Abba Father. We have the opportunity to talk to our Daddy calling it prayer. Jesus paid our atonement (penalty).

Now we know the importance of prayer. Lets view the relationship of Prayer and the Early Church. "These all continued with one accord in prayer and supplication, with the women and Mary the mother of Jesus, and with his brethren," Acts 1:14 We must remember that these 120 people became the leaders of the early church. These people, men and women, followed Jesus' instruction to stay in Jerusalem and wait for the Promise. They continued with one focus and purpose of prayer together as one unit. They did not know how long they would be praying. Jesus instructed 500 people to stay in Jerusalem and wait for the Promise stated in 1 Corinthians 15:6. What happened to the 380 people that did not go to the Upper Room? They made other choices and lived with the decision ten days later when the Promise (Holy Spirit) came.

After Holy Spirit was apart of their lives and very being, they continued praying (talking to the Father). "And they continued stedfastly in the apostles' doctrine and fellowship, and is breaking of bread and in prayers." Acts 2:42 They continued to follow what Jesus taught. They continued working as a unit in agreement with Christian principles and prayers.

The Bible records the apostles going to the temple at the hour of prayer, showing respect and living a lfestyle of corporate prayer in Acts 3:1 The apostles did not want to be distracted from the success of the early church. They were aware that continued growth of Christianity and supernatural manifestations were predicated upon prayer. "But we will give ourselves continually to prayer, and to the ministry of the word." Acts 6:4

It excited me in the ninth chapter of Acts that Saul was praying for help from his physical and spiritual blindness. What? Saul was trained by Gamaliel, one of the greatest teachers of the law. He was a Jewish rabbi and a leader in the Sanhedrin Council. Prayer was different for Saul now because he had a personal encounter with Grace (Jesus). He is now talking and making petitions to the Father in the Name of Grace, not the Law. Law is about works and demands. Grace is a gift and supplies.

As a young child I witnessed my mother exercise her faith in the power of prayer. While walking down the hallway in our home, I would hear my mother praying. She would be on her knees throughout the day in her bedroom talking to God. I heard her pray for family, our local church, friends, problems, world issues, etc. I would quietly go to another part of the house. I did not want to interrupt my mother's conversation. As I became older, I gained appreciation for my prayer warrior mother. She prayed daily with God resulting in successes that we are still enjoying today.

I witnessed my father sitting in his favorite lawn chair near the open barbecue pit in the backyard talking to God. My father was a deacon in our local fellowship which included public prayer in the meetings. My parents prayed and encouraged their children to talk with Father God, believing a little talk with Jesus made things right.

I never get tired of watching and experiencing the power of prayer in action. "Peter therefore was kept in prison: but prayer was made without ceasing of the church unto God for him." Acta 12:5 The believers were consistently praying as a unit with one purpose - Peter's release from jail. In verse 9, Peter was freed from jail with angelic visitation. Supernatural intervention was the result of their prayers.

"And when they had fasted and prayed, and laid their hands on them, they sent them away." Acts 13:3 In the Antioch Church, the early church leaders (prophets and teachers) after fasting and praying were instructed by the Holy Ghost to ordain Barnabas and Saul for the work of the ministry. They did nothing before praying and getting intel from Father God.

We are commanded to pray. Men ought always to pray according to Luke 18:1. Why? According to Matthew 26:41, we are taught to watch and pray that we do not enter into temptation. Prayer is our method used to receive from God. James 4:2 says, "we have not because we ask not." There is joy in prayer as stated in John 16:24. When I talk to my Father, I am never rushed. He never interrupts or ignores me. He listens and I always feel a release from heaviness. I know I can talk anytime I desire. I can stay as long as I choose. My speech and attire are not judged.

Prayer delivers us out of trouble. Psalm 34:6 Effective prayer unlocks the treasure of God's wisdom as stated in James 1:5. Remember James, the Callus Knee Preacher and half-brother of Jesus, experienced prayer that worked. He unlocked the treasure of God's wisdom. I remind myself daily that I know nothing, however I have access to Holy Spirit. He lives inside of me and knows everything. Throughout each day, I ask Holy Spirit for help and He unlocks the treasure of God's wisdom to me. During this COVID-19 pandemic perhaps everybody will come to the same conclusion, we know NOTHING. When we seek answers through Holy Spirit, this too shall pass. Holy Spirit can help us if we allow Him. Church, stop blogging, lets sit and listen.

"Call unto me. and I will answer thee, and show thee great and mighty things, which thou knowest not." Jeremiah 33:3 Prayer is our channel of communion. Our Father can not lie. Titus 1:2 He invited us to come to Him, speak our requests and He will answer us. He promised to show us great and might things. We do not know anything about these great and mighty things. Just imagine having access to the wisdom of God. When I was in college, my pastor and his wife took special interest in my welfare. They drove me to church weekly and I spent days at their home with other college students. We would read, pray, talk and study the Word. It was a Utopia, being in the company of like minded Christians. I think I believed all was possible. To my illusion upon graduation and separation from these people, I faced the real and cruel world once again. It was during my beginning investigative quest years for the early church that I learned the difference between church people and Christians.

I witnessed saved people demonstrating carnal behavior without guilt. These people attended church gatherings regularly, participated in church activities, however compromised christian principles often in their behavior. On the surface, they appeared to be applying christian principles, however they were straddling the fence between worldly behavior and a christian lifestyle. I heard about people of all ages, ethnicities and both genders partying with excessive alcohol, premarital sex, adultery, profanity, domestic violence etc. on Saturday nights. They were leaders in the local congregation on Sunday mornings preaching, teaching and leading praise and worship.

Dr. Katherine, are you saying that believers have to be perfect? No, all of us have sinned and fallen short of the glory of God according to Romans 3:23. Knowing we are not saved by works, but by grace. We must allow the Word of God to teach and develop us in Christian principles. All of us need continuous teaching. As individuals, we should embrace spiritual training by anointed leaders guided by Holy Spirit. Decades I coined this phrase; Be an active practicing Christian. This behavior satisfying the flesh is practiced by lay ministers as well as fivefold ministers. Church people do not actively and continuously practice christian lifestyles. They practice the lifestyle when it is convenient to their situation, cause or purpose.

Christians are chasing a closer and deeper relationship with the Father. They do not comdemn others, however choose to walk with others and lead by example. They are dying daily to their natural, carnal and earthly desires. They know a great price was paid for them at the Cross and pleasing the Father is their focus.

During my college years, I was fortunate and blessed to witness my pastor practice a christian lifestyle through prayer. Every night at 9:00 p.m. he would disappear regardless of schedules or guests. He would spend at least one hour alone in prayer. He had a special place in his home where he met with the Lord. His wife remarked that he had been doing this everyday since he was called to the office of pastor. I witnessed his action as a college student. Years later my family and I spent three days at his home and he was still practicing this behavior. This was his lifestyle.

I do not have that discipline. I pray several times during the day, however practicing a timed regime of prayer is admirable. I applaud his behavior and discipline of scheduled prayer time with our Father. He and his wife are approximately five years older than me. They attended a different undergraduate school from me; however their five children attended the same college as I did. Prayer is such a great and powerful tool.

Jesus believed in the power of praying. "And in that day ye shall ask me nothing. Verily, verily. I say unto you, Whatsoever ye shall ask the Father in my name, he will give it you. Hitherto have ye asked nothing in my name: ask, and ye shall receive, that your joy may be full." John 16: 23-24 He left the Church a message. Pray to God and ask in His name. Jesus is our Password. We pray in the name of Jesus because Jesus' sacrifice on Calvary gave us access to the Father. John 14: 13-14

We pray to our Father in heaven because He is our Creator, Owner, Father and is Omniscient, (knows everything); Ommipotent (has all power) and is Omnipresent (is everywhere). "Thou art worthy O Lord to receive power, honor and glory. For thou hast created all things and all things were and are created for your pleasure." Revelation 4:11 The One and Only One who created us wants to talk to us. He created prayer as our method of speaking with Him. He is our daddy (Abba Father)and we are his children. He loves hearing from us anytime and any place.

What were the prayers of the Early Church? In the book of Acts, we learn about the history of the early church prayers. They often gathered as a group to share and pray. They prayed for boldness to be representatives of the Church. They wanted strength to keep speaking about Jesus, in spite of the beatings, arrests and possible death. They prayed for health isues and saw healing. They prayed for salvations, signs, wonders, deliverances and miracles. The answers to their prayers manifested.

Dr. Katherine, I pray and never get my answers. Lets effectively pray. What? I teach and practice two methods of effective praying. "The effectual fervent prayer of a righteous man availeth much." James 5:16 This verse reminds us that our requests and petitions have great worth while communing and fellowshiping with God. Because we are the Righteousness of God in Jesus Christ based on Jesus finished work at the Cross, our prayers result in the desired answers.

The first method of effectve praying is Praying in the Holy Spirit. "God is a Spirit and they that worship Him must worship Him in Spirit and in truth." John 4:24 My native language is English, however I am able to read and speak in some degree in French. My communication preference is English and anyone desiring a suitable outcome to a request from me would have to speak to me in English. Since our Heavenly Father is a Spirit, it would be wise to pray in the Spirit when speaking to Him. Holy Spirit knows what to say while using our vocal cords in audible speech.

What if I do not know what I am saying when I am praying in the Spirit? GREAT!!! Many times, we do not know what to pray. We do not want to pray our own will, therefore we pray in the Spirit. Holy Spirit is perfect and knows the perfect prayer to pray. Romans 8: 26-27 says "Likewise the Spirit also helpeth our infirmities; for we know not what we should pray for as we ought, but the Spirit itself maketh intercession for us with groaning which cannot be uttered. And He that searcheth the hearts knoweth what is the mind of the Spirit, because He maketh intercession for the saints according to the will of God." Church, we must pray in the Holy Spirit. We must pray in tongues and use our prayer language daily.

I craved praying in tongues for years. I never thought it was outdated or works of the devil. I did not know how to receive this gift. I listened to church leaders in 'Holiness and Pentecostal Churches'. These leaders said." You must tarry for this gift. You do not want it enough." After a Sunday evening service at a Pentecostal Church, I stayed about four hours as they prayed for me for my prayer language in tongues. I was so tired. They were holding up my arms. Some of these leaders had not used their prayer language in years. Some believed that I was not going to heaven if I did not have the gift. I knew that was a lie and told them. I knew I was saved and going to heaven. I did not need to pray in tongues in heaven, but I sure did need my prayer language on earth. I was the poster child of a defeated Christian. I could have faked sounds so I could go home and they would not know the difference. My love and reverence for God would not allow me to fake this gift. I left that fellowship.

My younger daughter was the first in our immediate family to receive the gift of praying in tongues. In a Sunday evening service, she received the gift. I asked her what happened because I wanted to repeat her actions to receive the gift. I had been begging and pleading for the gift. My daughter advised me to cease begging and pleading and just receive my prayer language. This gift was not hiding from me.

The next year in a Tuesday night small rural interdenominational church prayer meeting, the following happened: the pastor spoke in tongues as well as most of the group. She would say at each meeting, "If you can not pray in tongues, just pray in your native language. I would pray in English. I was very comfortable there. I did not feel any pressure or feel judged. This particular night she said, "If you can not speak in tongues, keep quiet. Everybody who can speak in tongues, use your prayer language now." For a few seconds, I felt alone and left out. For a few minutes, I listened to them praying in other languages; then I opened my mouth and this unknown language in me came forth. That was decades ago and I am so happy that I am no longer defeated. I agree with Apostle Paul and thank God that I speak in tongues. I thank God for His unspeakable gift and rejoice with joy for this gift that I can not adequately express appreciation for and full of glory. 2 Corinthians 9:15; 1 Peter 1:8 For decades, both of my daughters and I use our prayer language daily. Hallelujah!

What if I do not pray in Tongues? If you want the Gift of Praying in Tongues, ask God and He will freely give you the Gift. Praying in Tongues is for all. Acts 2: 38-39. When I began praying in tongues, I described it as follows: Before receiving this gift, I prayed in English and quoted the scripture. I was limited because I did not know the root of the issue that I was making the petition. When I use my prayer language, I do not need to know the root. Holy Spirit, Who is praying through me, knows all things and goes to the root, eliminates it and the correct answer manifests.

The second method of effective prayer is praying the Word. God is His Word. He honors Himself. He is in agreement with His Word, Himself. We should pray the Word of God back to Him. Although God is a Spirit, He knows His Word. Choose scriptures from the Bible that correspond with your need or request and pray it back to God. God encourages us to put Him in remembrance of His promises. It is not because He does not remember His promises. It puts us in remembrance of the Covenant that we have with Father, Who is always faithful and can not lie.

I start my prayers in my native language. I end my prayers in tongues. I know that I do not know the real issue. Since I am speaking with my limited understanding in the natural, I like to pray in tongues longer than I do in English. This is my method of allowing Holy Spirit to correct my prayer and impart wisdom to me about my prayer. Using this method, I remove my flesh from the interaction and receive from the Spirit.

I am certified to teach night watches and soaking prayer. I have facilitated several night watches for believers in several states. It is a twelve hour period, beginning at 6:00 p.m. and ending at 6:00 a.m. These watches are divided into four segments of three hours each. We pray during these sessions for specific requests. We are in prayer agreement and have witnessed answered prayers as the result. Soaking prayer is a quiet time before the Lord in a safe and protective environment. During this time, participants open up to intimacy and allows Father to lead and set us free. It positions all before the Lord for acceptance and love from the Father. Soaking removes all inhibitions and vulnerabilities. Each session should have a certified soaking prayer minister to guide the participants with scripture and worship music. I have witnessed cries, laughter, quietness, stillness and wailing during soaking times. Expect an intimate encounter without knowing the result of the soaking. Be still my soul. Take time regardless of minutes or hours to relax in His presence. Give Holy Spirit permission to minister to you. Accept the wisdom of you not knowing what will happen. Give up control and surrender to the Only One Who is Wisdom and will protect us as we are transformed to a new vessel. Then, we are refreshed and energized.

"I decree and declare that the fire, faith and power of the Early Church has been restored in today's Church in Jesus Name" prays Dr. Katherine. Is this possible? Yes, Jesus Christ, the same yesterday, today and forever. Our Father does not change. His power is still available to those who believe and walk by faith and not by sight. One of the goals of this book is to stir the fire in believers (the Church) to pray, believe, decree and reject anything less than the Salvation Plan Jesus purchased for us on the Cross. "Death and life are in the power of the tongue. Those that love it, eat the fruit thereof." Proverbs 18:21 Speak what you expect and receive the benefits.

Hallelujah!

Praise and Worship

"I will bless the LORD at all times: his praise
shall continually be in my mouth."

PSALM 34:1

When I was a college student, I enrolled in an elective course in Physical Education. I chose badminton because of the limited choices during the Summer Session. I was unfamiliar with this sport. Badminton was not offered in my high school and I did not have any friends who played this sport. As a female, I ran track, played softball, basketball, volleyball and watched football, tennis and golf.

This Summer Course of Badminton was three and one-half weeks long. This was a coed class, lasting ninety minutes five days weekly. All of the students and the coach instructor, excluding me, were white Americans. All of them were familiar with badminton. Some participated in this sport in their recreational courts as well as their backyards. The coach instructor did not explain the basic fundamentals of the game. He took for granted that everyone in the class was familiar with this sport. Although I take pride in being a good athlete, I lost every match and was highly embarrassed.

One hot summer afternoon, my college friend came to visit me. She was not enrolled in the Summer Session, but was a Physical Education major. She and I were basketball players for the college. She knew I was a gifted athlete. I shared with her my plight, expressing that I was being stomped. Hearing my frustration, she walked with me to the gymnasium. We played the game of badminton for less than a minute and she assessed my problem. She shared with me the basic fundamentals of the game. What did I not know? What was I doing wrong? I was hitting the birdie directly to my opponent, instead of away from my opponent. A light went off in my head and the game was simple. The next day was the finals. It was labeled a Double Elimination Final, meaning you had to lose twice. I took the court and won every match. At the end of the ninety minute session, I was standing undefeated with a male opponent. What was the difference? I had the knowledge required for success in badminton. My Father sent his child and my friend for an unexpected visit. All of my life I had heard, He is never too late, but right on time. Some would say He may come at midnight, but He comes. Daddy sent my friend the afternoon before Finals.

I use this true story from my life often to share that sometimes we simply do not know the rules, fundamentals or purpose of certain things. When I was a high school teacher, I carefully took time to explain each exercise and assignment to the students. Later as a mother, I took time to explain activities to my children. This day as a Fivefold Ministry Teacher and Christian Minister, I take time to explain the Word of God to all listeners. I have never forgotten feeling inadequate and embarassed because the coach instructor took for granted that all of the badminton students knew the game. I follow this principle in every aspect of my life. Do people know or understand the basic fundamentals or principles of marriage, family, parenting, etc.?

Practicing this principle, I am confident of having better success in our lives. God made us because He wanted a family. He had and still has a purpose for His family. What is the problem? Many in the Body of Christ have never been taught His purpose for His Creation. Others in the Body of Christ refuse to accept their purpose.

God's original plan for us consisted of a shared authority and ruling class of people. It was never His intent that we become servants. The first gift that He gave to us was His image and likeness. He wanted us to be like Him. Doesn't this sound like a loving parent? How many of us want our children to look and act like us and have some of our mannerisms. I find myself blushing with pride while smiling when I witness my fingerprint in my daughters and grandchild whether it manifests in speech or behavior.

God wanted us close to Him. He wanted us in His presence. In the Hebrew language, Eden refers to a place of God's presence. Where did God place His creation? Eden was the ideal place. God's desire for a family provoked the angels to ask questions in Psalm 8. This speaking being wanted to know why this creature called Adam was so important to God. After all, God had a perfect environment according to this being.

God was consistently offered genuine praise. The devil had been kicked out of heaven for his disobedience, jealousy and defiance. This angel wanted to know why God wanted this inferior creature called man. The angel inquired as to why God thought of this creature so much and why did God visit this creature. Let's make it plain: This speaking being-angel-had witnessed God visiting Adam in the cool of the day as recorded in Genesis 3:8. This angel wanted to know why God had given this creation power over all things in the earth. It puzzled this angel that God created angels to be ministers and heavenly messengers unto this creature.

What the angel failed to know was God's desire for a family that would have a will of its own. This new creature could accept or reject His Creator. There are blessings and curses for the choice: however, the choice is there. Who was this new creature? Us, we are the new creature. We were created to be His family. Now, we must understand our purpose. We will not have any "badminton" errors. The intent of this writing is to explain in detail our purpose as creation in relationship to His intent for us as Creator. This is knowledge that the Early Church embraced as their new lifestyle.

Did you know that we were created for one purpose and only one purpose? What is the purpose for our existence? Revelation 4:11 tells us that God created all things and that includes all of us. All of his creations were made for one purpose and that purpose is HIS

PLEASURE. Let's make it plain: Man, woman, girl and boy were created to please God. Times have not changed. Hebrews 13:8 says. "Jesus Christ, the same yesterday, and today, and for ever." In Psalm 102:18, God said, "This shall be written for the generation to come: and the people which shall be created shall praise the Lord." Written for generations to come: that is US. God said let them know that they are and were created to praise ME.

Praise has been described as cheering, applauding and clapping for our Father. Worship has been described as kissing our Father, an intimate touch with our lips to our Creator. Our lips open and we speak, sing and shout words of adoration and love to the GREATEST. When describing Praise, it is not What. Praise is Who! I am expressing my personal appreciation for GOD'S GREATNESS. I am thinking of and choosing to get lost in adoration and the deepest love that I have ever encountered for my Father, Who loves me just as I am. I can lie down, stand, sit, kneel, run, walk, etc. and my posture is received. I can laugh, cry, shout, moan, grunt, talk, shout or remain silent in my Praise. My position, posture and speech can be determined according to my setting or location. My personal and private time is so valuable to me because I do not have any spectators or distractors. This is my time with my Father as I enjoy His presence and express my love and appreciation for the purity that He gives to me.

As a child, I understood praise to be fast songs with a rhythmic beat and Worship to be slow songs with empathy. A traditional service began with two praise songs followed by three worship songs before the Sermon Hymn. The hymn preceded the message. It was the song that was slow and used to engage the congregation before the Word was preached. After decades of this practice, I realized that I had difficulty entering into praise and worship with other groups. I was confused. Where are the fast, slow and slower songs to prepare me for the Word? I do not know the words or melody of these songs. These songs are not familiar to me.

I enjoyed praise and worship in my denomination and familiar surroundings. We sang songs that lifted and rejuvenated us. My mother was the president of our local church choir. She wrote songs and sang solos often. She had a beautiful voice that captivated the listener which resulted in all joining in the singing. I did not inherit her gift of singing, however I make a joyful noise through praise and worship.

I was attending the Brownsville Revival in Florida and scheduled to be there for three days. I was having a miserable time. I could not "tap in". I was looking around the auditorium and watching others enjoy their time with the Lord. I was thinking what if they sing this song or that song then I can join in. That evening, I telephoned my daughters and asked if they were praying for me. They assured me they were and I went into detail about my dissatisfaction. They listened saying they would continue to pray while believing my experience would change to satisfaction and enjoyment.

My traveling companion was a fivefold minister pastor. I decided to confide in her. I asked whether she was enjoying the Revival? She said yes. I asked do you know the songs they are singing? She said no. We were good friends and of different ethnicities. The majority of the people in the Revival Services were of her ethnicity. I quickly asked, "What are you singing during Praise and Worship? It seems like you "tap in" and enjoy yourself". She smiled and said, "If I know the song, I sing the words. If I do not know the song, I sing my words to the Father".

A light went off in my head that could have provided electricity for a city block. I prayed in my hotel room that night, repenting and praising my Father for the next day's service. I was ready early to go to the service. We attended about three services daily. When the music began, I was ready to "tap in". I thoroughly enjoyed praise and worship and was familiar with only one of the chosen songs. Thank you Father and my friend for sharing with me. Since that day and hour, I can enter into praise and worship with all peoples regardless of ethnicity or language as long as it is CHRISTIAN. If it is not Christianity, we do not have a common bond. Without the mutual foundation of Jesus, I can not praise nor worship it. My praise and worship is reserved for and freely given to THE ONLY ONE WORTHY OF ALL - ELOHIM-GOD, ALMIGHTY CREATOR!

Although I have shared the above story for decades, I know there are many Christians who have the same problem. I have Christian friends who have shared that they have difficulty worshiping with other denominations and ethnicities. They remark that they do not like the music or the people can not sing. They are conditioned to certain patterns and styles of praise and worship that limit their experience with the Presence of the Father. I have participated and enjoyed praise and worship of a language I do not understand. I practice and enjoy Father's presence which opens the door. We should teach believers to praise and worship the Creator and not the words or rhythm of the music.

I enjoy praise and worship experiences with my husband. He gets lost in his time fellowshiping with Father. He is unaware of others, including me. He interacts with his heavenly Father with love, awe and great appreciation of Who His Creator is. During his praise and worship, whether he is in his car, at home or in public meetings; he is in tune with his Abba Daddy. His relationship with his Father shows up in the natural through joyful expressions of lifted hands, dance, claps, amens, tears, kneeling, etc.

Because of my husband's unapologetic expression of his praise and worship, I have witnessed men coming to him after services expressing their desire to become open and free. He shares with them about his appreciation and gratitude of God loving him. Usually we sit in the back of fellowship gatherings so we can express ourselves without being a spectacle to others. What? We want everybody to focus their attention to the Father leading to their freedom and His glory.

I praise God daily for Who He IS. He is EVERYTHING GREAT AND GOOD. I take time to remind myself of my Father's Being. First, God is THE DIVINE SUPREME BEING WHO operates without the assistance of mankind. What does this mean to me? God predates His creation and is NOT dependent upon His creation, however His creation is dependent upon Him. Second, I choose to focus on the Names of God as I praise Him. One of my favorite names to praise Him is ANCIENT OF DAYS, reminding me that He predates All. He is AGELESS and TIMELESS.

Excuse me while I take this moment to praise Him. "The Only One Who is greater than time, the One Who is Everlasting from Everlasting, First and Last, Alpha and Omega, The One Who was and Who Is and Who Is to Come, The Beginning and the Ending. The One is Omnipotent, Omnipresent and Omniscient loves and accepts me as His child. There is NO ONE or NOTHING that He loves more than me." These are just words until I take time to meditate on each word, which can take several minutes or hours to appreciate and thank my Father, Abba Pater, my Daddy for loving me.

As I am writing this, today is the anniversary date of my mother's eternal flight to Glory. To be absent from the body is to be present with the Lord. I praise God daily that my mother is in His presence. I have completed 365 days on earth without my mother. This past year has been a different experience for me. I did not lose my mother. She is not lost. I have her address. I do not physically see or talk to her, however I consistently talk about her. I am so grateful for my Christian heritage.

If we can get physically excited at sporting events and secular activities of our choosing, what prevents us from praising the Only One worthy of our praise? We are ungrateful, selfish and lazy people. If you have thought or said,"It does not take all that to praise God. I like quiet, dignified services." Let's make it plain: You have just worked with the devil. The devil does not care what we think, just does not want us to praise God. Every time we refuse or carelessly do not give God praise, we have made a choice to be on satan's side by agreeing with him that God is not worthy of praise. God forbid! We know that God is worthy to be praised. When we gather as Christians, we should praise God. "My foot standeth in an even place: in the congregations will I bless the Lord." (Psalm 26:12) As we gather in large groups, "I will give thanks in the great congregation: I will praise thee among much people." (Psalm 35:18) The larger the crowd, the more praise comes forth. In an atmosphere of agreement, we praise God.

We must come out of bondage. Being shy and embarassing to praise God is a form of bondage. This bondage benefits the devil.

We must make a declaration of release from bondage in our praise. Psalm 107:32 says, "Let them exalt Him also in the congregation of the people and praise Him in the assembly of the elders." Do you remember Jesus' Triumphant Entry into Jerusalem on what we now call Palm Sunday? The Scripture says the whole multitude cried out praising and rejoicing Jesus in a loud voice for all the mighty works that they had witnessed. Some of the Pharisees asked Jesus to rebuke them for their shameful behavior. Jesus said, "If these should hold their peace, the stones would immediately cry out." Luke 19:40 Do we want stones to cry out about His mighty works? God forbid!

God said. "This people have I formed for myself; they shall show forth my praise" in Isaiah 42:21. God is saying I created you, made you and formed you for myself. I created you to please Me and praising Me is My pleasure. Happiness will forever be a stranger for those who do not practice a lifestyle of praise. Why? We are and were created to praise our Creator. Fill the vacuum in your heart with Praise for the Father.

Peter had an intimate relationship with Jesus and thought He was worthy of praise. Peter reminds us that. "We are a chosen generation, a royal priesthood, a holy nation, a peculiar people; that we should show forth the praises of him who hath called us out of darkness into His marvelous light." (1 Peter 2:9)

Sisters and brothers, I am taking a moment to reflect upon His Goodness. "Thank you, Lord, for calling us out of the darkness into Your marvelous light. We are a purchased people bought with a price. We have been purchased to praise the One who called us out. We did not know just how lost we were until You came for us. You called us out of our dark, dying and hopeless state. You chose us as your people. We realize that You chose us first; however, we gladly accept your invitation to dine at Your table. We love you SOOOOOOO much Daddy!" If we would take time to show forth His praise, we would reach higher levels of intimacy in the Body of Christ, What were we called to do? Our answer is locked up in our praise.

God commanded His creation to praise Him. Psalm 150 instructs us to praise Him in the Church; praise Him for His power, His mighty acts and praise Him with musical instruments. If we want to please God, we must first learn just what pleases Him. God says in Psalm 150:6, "Let everything that hath breath praise the Lord." Let's make it plain: If we are breathing, praise the Lord.

Praise pleases God more than an offering. Psalm 69: 30-31 says, "I will praise the name of God with a song, and will magnify Him with thanksgiving. This also shall please the Lord better than an ox or bullock that hath horns and hoofs." Let's open our mouths and cheerfully give God all praise that He is worthy of.

How do we praise our Creator? Praise takes many biblical forms. Some of the forms include singing, shouting, making a joyful noise, laughter, thanksgiving, standing, kneeling, clapping, dancing, uplifted hands, speaking and singing in tongues and making noise on instruments. Although praise takes many forms, it is always visible and audible. Praise cannot be hidden or kept silent. In the Old Testament, we learn about an emotional and expressive people. They were not afraid to openly show how they felt about God. Celebration and exhilaration were regularly part of their worship. As Psalm 150 instructs us, we must praise God with our whole being.

God surrounds Himself in our praise. "But thou art holy, O thou that inhabitest the praises of Israel." (Psalm 22:3) When we are despondent and feel hopeless and do not think God is listening, what is the answer?" Go where He lives! His address is Praise. He lives and dwells in praise. There is power in Praise. Call on Judah and mean it with every fiber of your being and witness the supernatural power of God enter the situation. Praise draws on God's personality. When God is showered and pleased with praise, He comes down in person. His coming down and showing up in the middle of your praise changes everything. Have you ever experienced His Holy Presence in the middle of your situation? You will cry, weep, shake, appear paralyzed, dance, sit still, holler, shout, sometimes lie still, fall down and become speechless, etc. when His Holy Presence invades your space.. He invades in different forms, so we cannot predict His method. We know He is coming because He loves and enjoys true and genuine praise.

A Praise Break is coming: "Father, swallow me up with your presence. We love You and everything is right when You visit us. There is no one like You. You are worthy of all praise. How great is thy faithfulness! Who is like You? NO ONE!"

Man was created to live and function in the presence of God. Praise is the ideal environment for man and creation. Praise attracts the presence of God, maintains the presence of God and is a prerequisite for the presence of God. Complaining and murmuring guarantee the absence of God's presence. How many of us long to be in the presence of complaining, whining and needy people? None. Nothing is less desirable than surrounding ourselves with ungrateful, selfish and murmurimg people.

When we praise God with our lips and our hearts, He shows His approval and acceptance by manifesting His presence in our midst. This is the main ingredient for true worship. His presence releases His glory. Praise is agreeing with God concerning Himself. We are taking time to brag on the Only One who deserves the praise. When we praise Him, we are telling Him all the good and wonderful things about Himself. Praise is boasting on God's nature, attributes and character. True praise comes only from a humble heart that is focused on God. Try focusing on God which will always result in some form of praise.

Psalm 92: 1-5 says, "It is a good thing to give thanks unto the Lord, and to sing praises unto thy name, O Most High: to show forth thy loving-kindness in the morning, and thy faithfulness every night, upon an instrument of ten strings, and upon the psaltery; upon the harp with a solemn sound. For thou Lord, hast made me glad through thy work: I will triumph in the works of thy hands. O Lord, how great are thy works! And thy thoughts are very deep." Praise should be freely given to our Creator.

Is there any regularity to my praise? Is praising Him during Church services enough? Psalm 34:1 says, "I will bless the Lord at all times: His praise shall continually be in my mouth." Let's make it plain: His creation, meaning us, should praise God all the time. Praise Him at home, work, school, leisure time, devotion, praying, driving, church, etc. Our praise is NOT limited to the activities listed. Praise Him all the time.

There is not a special time to praise Him. Psalm 113:3 says, "From the rising of the sun unto the going down of the same, the Lord's name is to be praised." Praising God all day for His Goodness is the song on our lips. We should "Praise the name of the Lord: for His name alone is excellent; His glory is above the earth and heaven." (Psalm 148:13)

When we are happy, we should praise our Creator. "Is any merry? Let him sing psalms." (James 5:13) The psalms are songs written to tell the history of Israel and are called the "Book of Praises." Choose a psalm of praise and sing it to the Lord. Our new song should focus on all God is and has done for us. "Sing to the Lord a new song for He has done marvelous things: His right hand and His holy arm have worked salvation for Him." (Psalm 98:1)

When we do not feel like praising God, we are commanded to praise Him anyway. Why? Praise has nothing to do with our feelings. Times may be good; times may be bad. This does not change our relationship with our Daddy, Almighty God. Once we find the secret dwelling place of God in the midst of our praise, we go to Him day and night. "Why art thou cast down, O my soul? And why art thou disquieted within me? Hope thou in God: for I shall yet praise Him, who is the health of my countenance, and my God." (Psalm 42:11) The psalmist did not blame God for his condition, therefore he commanded his soul to praise the Only One who could change the status quo.

What do we praise Him for? 1 Thessalonians 5:18 says, "In every thing gives thanks: for this is the will of God in Christ Jesus concerning you." In all situations, we must give thanks. The scripture does not say give thanks for everything. When a tragedy comes in our lives, we do not praise God for the tragedy. We praise God for Who He is in our lives during the tragedy and thanks for guiding us through the crisis.

We make a choice to set our will and emotions to praise God regardless of feelings and circumstances. We remember Psalm 42:5

and with praise, our spirit man rises up and tells depression and heaviness to loose us, and we are supernaturally released. Leviticus 22:29 says, "And when ye will offer a sacrifice of thanksgiving unto the Lord, offer it at your own will." Sometimes we have to offer praise when we do not feel like it or there does not appear to be any reason for thanks or praise. When we press through with praise, our feelings, circumstances and viewpoint change suddenly. We know without a shadow of doubt that our Redeemer, Who has never forsaken us is alive. We are shouting Hallelujah praises all over the place. The atmosphere changes and now miracles can happen. Hallelujah - Praise God - You are so Worthy.

The praise comes from. "I can do all things through Christ which strengtheneth me." (Philippians 4:13) We praise the Only One Who is able to sustain us, Jesus Christ, the Anointed One and His Anointing. God's original intent for us, His creation, is simple. We are to wake up in His presence, work in His presence, talk in His presence, play in His presence, eat in His presence, cry in His presence, laugh in His presence, dance in His presence and go to sleep in His presence. Every activity in our lives is to be comfortable in His presence. Why do we shy away from Him? Why do we fear the One who loves us so much? Why can't we cry, "Come, Lord, come and visit me, stay awhile and talk with me?" Many of us do not have a relationship with our Creator and do not know how to approach Him.

Psalm 103: 1-4 says. "Bless the Lord, O my soul: and all that is within me, bless His Holy name. Bless the Lord, O my soul and forget not all His benefits. Who forgiveth all thine iniquities; Who healeth all thy diseases; Who redeemeth thy life from destruction; Who crowneth thee with lovingkindness and tender mercies." What does the Scripture mean by "Bless?" The word means expressions of praise, adoration and appreciation for the Lord in whatever way we choose.

What is the soul? We are created in three parts. We are spirit, we have a soul and we live in a body. We are spirit, soul and body. The spirit man never dies, grows from the Word of God and communicates with God. The soul is our will, intellect, emotions, personality and thoughts. We are housed and live in a body that is flesh and blood and will never be saved. We must instruct our soul to praise God.

Stop and take a Praise Break: Lift hands and praise God for Who He is and What He has, is and will do in our lives. Give thanks for His work in our lives - past, present and future. I call this action, Practicing His Presence.

Some believers think praising God is the key to getting everything they want. We cannot fool God. God knows sincere praise. He knows our motives and He responds accordingly. False praise does not honor God. He will not show up when our motives are less than honorable. God says in Isaiah 29:13. "These people come near to Me with their mouth and honor Me with their lips, but their hearts are far from Me. Their worship of Me is made up only of rules taught by men." What did God mean? Fake worship, somebody devised a formula of worship to "con" God. Are we smarter than our Creator? Is it possible to deceive the One who created us? God forbid!

Worship is equally important to the lifestyle of a believer. In worship, the believer is loving, admiring, adoring and appreciating the Father for His holiness. Christians enter worship in a state of intimacy expressing and experiencing the Father one on one. It is our personal encounter where we give all that we are to all that He is. There in no greater intimacy. Speaking as one who loves her husband; worship is a higher level than the physical intimacy shared in a loving marriage.

In a holy matrimonial union, the husband and wife explore deep and deeper levels of physical intimacy throughout their relationship. In worship, the believer explores levels of spiritual intimacy which renders one completely naked before our Father. We are not embarassed and allow Him to clothe us with Himself which manifests in the natural as love for mankind. The Book of Song of Solomon describes worship better than any illustration known to me. When we take time to worship Him with all we have and enter the Holy of Holies (the anointed place that WAS behind the veil and NOW accessible to every believer); we find Him sitting and waiting for us. He is there waiting to talk and listen to us, He has the HELP that we need and desire. We do not have to make an appointment. Come with sincerity and there our Father sits smiling and ready to embrace us. The Song of Solomon 1:2 says, "Let Him kiss me with the kisses of His mouth: for thy love is better than wine." We kiss His face in our praise. We are kissing the One Who will never disappoint or betray us.

Times of Worship are so valuable. True worship changes us and we long for special moments, which can be hours, of sitting or lying in His presence. Take a moment to think about THE ONLY ONE WHO IS PERFECT; KNOWS EVERYTHING ABOUT EVERYBODY AND ALL THINGS; CREATED EVERY GOOD THING AND HAS FORGIVEN ALL BELIEVERS OF PAST, PRESENT AND FUTURE SINS chooses to spend time with us. We can choose the QUANTITY (amount) of time which is ALWAYS QUALITY (effectiveness) with Father. We are ALWAYS BETTER for the time we spend with Father.

When true worship is the initiator, Father comes in His glory. Praise bids Him come and worship ushers His presence. Can you recall the atmosphere in which God showed up in the Philippian jail? "About midnight Paul and Silas were praying and singing hymns to God, and the other prisoners were listening to them. Suddenly there was such a violent earthquake that the foundations of the prison were shaken. At once all the prison doors flew open, and everybody's chains came loose." (Acts 16: 25-26)

Paul and Silas did not think about their present surroundings. They knew that God did not put them in jail. They knew that God was worthy to be praised. They embraced the opportunity to preach and teach others about Jesus as a pleasure. They were anxious to spread the Good News, the Gospel, the News Too Good To Be True. They had been thrown in jail because they preached the Gospel in spite of being threatened with jail and beatings. They had the opportunity to whine and complain. They could have complained about the conditions in the jail. They could have whined about the size of the jail cell, the stench of the urine and bowel waste, disease infestation, the rats crawling and feasting on them. God forbid!

Paul and Silas were willing Christians. They were on the front line in Early Church ministry. They volunteered for service and took pride in their assignments. In jail, they made a choice to praise, worship and bless God through prayer and songs. They had a late night praise and worship meeting with the Father. Time, situation, nor place dictated their decision. The hymns and prayers flowed from their mouths. They knew their confinement was temporary. How temporal was it? The scripture says "suddenly, " meaning unexpectantly and quickly things changed.

As I practice praising and worshiping the Father, I become less concerned with personal and secular matters. I start to focus on what pleases the Father. My love, compassion and empathy for others increase each time I practice His presence. After these sessions that I crave, I lose my selfish desires and learn to minister to others without seeking self-gain. Each time the early church gathered with praise and worship for the Father; strength, encouragement and unity increased. The early church left every gathering with renewed vigor and commitment to do greater works for the Lord. Persecution, beatings and incarceration did not deter them. In Acts 4:20 after being threatened, Peter and John answered, "For we cannot but speak the things which we have seen and heard." What were they speaking? They were speaking the Good News of Jesus, praising Him for His Goodness and worshiping Him for His Holiness.

In Acts 5: 40-42, we read of the apostles being beaten and threatened to shut up talking about Jesus. The apostles took the beatings and received the threats, however left the council rejoicing that they were counted worthy to suffer shame for His name. They taught, preached, praised and worshiped daily in the temple and houses. What about us? We do not have to think about anybody beating us because of our love for the Father. We just refuse to praise God. We want to be in services that cater to our needs, thoughts and desires. I hear the following comments about church services: "They are too loud. They are mixing races. The building is in the wrong part of town. The people are plain and country. They look like drug people. Did you see all the tattoes? That is not my denomination. The last time I went there, Dr. Katherine took off running, Dr. Katherine embarasses me with her praise and worship. Now, what was that about? It was about praise! I was set free by God from emotional bondage and have been running since that day. I describe my actions as a wild horse, refusing a bridle and saddle. I will never have any person or situation dictating to me what is acceptable or tolerable when I am praising and worshiping my Father. When He freed me to run, I fled as one discovering, exploring and conquering new territories.

I do not apologize or even attempt to explain to mankind my relationship with God. Why? My relationship with my Father (God) is personal, intimate and All mine. It is special between us and we enjoy each other. I never forget that I was created for His pleasure and not the pleasure of mankind. I choose to praise Him with all of my being and refuse to apologize or alter the method that it might visualize or vocalize itself. I am chasing the Early Church by singing hymns, praising and worshiping our Father.

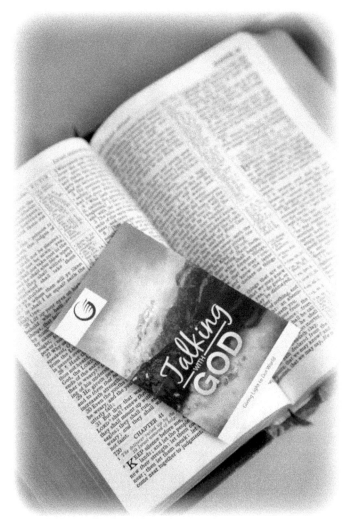

All of His Promises are True

Walking in
Divine Health

························◆························

*"Who his own self bare our sins in his own body on
the tree that we, being dead to sins, should live unto
righteousness: by whose stripes ye were healed."*

1 PETER 2:24

It is our annual Resurrection Season as I am writing. My country,
United States of America, is plagued with the corona virus (Covid
19) at this time in 2020. I was in the middle of writing when the
outbreak became a part of our daily lives. Although I confess that I
am the Righteousness of God in Jesus Christ because of His finished
work on the Cross and my acceptance of Jesus as my Savior, I also
plead the Blood of Jesus over my family, friends, dwelling and myself
daily.

I remember the promises that Jesus gave me in my Salvation
Package. One of my promises is Divine Health. God wants us well.
Can you imagine wanting your child or loved one sick? Can you
imagine putting sickness or diseases upon your child or loved one
to punish or teach lessons? I can not imagine any SANE person
behaving in this manner? Jesus said if we being evil know how to
give good gifts to our children, what about our Father in heaven. He
will give us good things when we ask. (Matthew 7:11)

I am extremely disappointed each time I hear people (even church leaders) saying God is putting sickness upon us. The Bible tells us that Jesus took our sins and sicknesses to the Cross. When Jesus was beat at the whipping post and scourged, each lash resulted in a stripe making a huge hole in his back was for us. I let myself imagine each stripe being a disease, sickness, weakness, infirmity, lack or death that was conquered by Jesus for me. Anything that I maybe dealing with or trying to affect my body, I deny its existence in or on my body because (1) it is a trespasser; (2) Jesus defeated this enemy on the Cross for me and (3) as Jesus is so am I (1John 4:17).

Some people believe that God placed the corona virus upon the United States and sent Hurricane Katrina to New Orleans as forms of judgment for legalized abortions, homosexual practices, etc. Church, listen carefully, the two examples used are sin. The God that I know (my Daddy) is not using Death as His ally or method of punishment or judgment. My Bible teaches me that Death is His enemy. " The last enemy that shall be destroyed is death." 1 Corinthians 15:26 Jesus is not imputing past, present nor future sins against us. (Hebrews 8:12) If the corona virus was sent by God to judge and punish the United States, why are other countries affected? Are these people saying that God, the Creator of this world, does not know the location of the United States? (Just a little humor) Was New Orleans the only city where sin was practiced in 2005? Why would God choose that city? GOD DID NOT AND WILL NOT SEND KATRINA OR ANY DEVASTATIONS TO KILL HIS PEOPLE. Is this Covid 19 one of the plagues mentioned in the book of Revelation? Plagues are recorded in Revelation, but this corona virus (Covid 19) is not one of those plagues. When those plagues appear, the church will have been raptured. Since I am still here and I know that I am a member of the church; that argument does not have merit.

Sisters and brothers, John 12:32 says "And I, if I be lifted up from the earth, will draw all men unto me". Jesus was speaking of His death by crucifixion stating that when He is lifted up on the Cross, He will draw all God's wrath to Him. Believers, stop accusing our Heavenly Father of judging America or any country for their sins. God took His judgment out on the body of Jesus on the Cross. Stop accusing our Heavenly Father of sending storms, fires, earthquakes and catastrophic events to teach us lesssons or punish us. Our Father loves us. He is not angry with us. God's wrath in the Old Testament was real. This wrath took place under the Law. We are no longer under the Law, we are under Grace because Jesus has paid our penalty for all our sins.

God is NOT angry with us. We received in our Salvation package the Covenant of Peace (Shalom). This covenant was purchased by the Blood of Jesus. As believers when we honor Jesus' sacrifice on the Cross, we see Him rising with healing in His wings as recorded in Malachi 4: 2. This healing covers all areas of our lives. Decades ago, I thought Jesus only delivered and healed our physical ailments. I was suffering from emotional hurts and did not know what to do. One day, I heard the truth from a gifted christian female who walked in the gift of healing. I believed what I heard because it was the truth (right there in the Bible). How had I missed this? I was saved at age eight and practiced a Christian lifestyle. I missed it because I had not searched the healing scriptures for myself. Since that day, I search the Scriptures in every area for myself. My teacher, mentor and guide through the scriptures is the Holy Spirit. He guides me in All truth. Now, I receive my Healing in all seven areas: Spiritually, Physically, Emotionally, Mentally, Pyschologically, Socially and Financially.

Sickness can come through open doors of sin in our lives due to our own actions, NOT GOD. When we open the door of sin, the devil steps in and takes a huge advantage. Sickness can come through devil attacks because of his hatred of God. The devil hates all believers who are the children of God. Our Father loves us. We live in a fallen world and the devil is trying to devour us. (1 Peter 5:8) We are in a spiritual battle with the devil, looking for an opportunity to steal, kill and destroy. (John 10:10) Sickness can also come from natural things. Have you ever twisted your ankle while walking or running? The result was a swollen or sprained ankle. Were you sinning or did the devil push you? When I was playing college basketball, while in the air trying to retreive a rebound, I twisted my body while landing, resulting in an awkward fall. Less than ten seconds my coach was on the court; the basketball trainer had to cut the tennis shoe off due to the rapid swelling of my right ankle. I was an athlete playing basketball, not committing a sin. The devil was not trying to beat me to the rebound. It was a natural athletic incident that happened during the game.

Our Father is the Lord that heals. The biblical word for healing is <u>refuah</u> from the root word, <u>rapha</u>. The Hebrew words that refer to heal or health also means to restore, repair, make healthy, prolong life, bind a wound and to heal all types of diseases. My right ankle was a wound being bound. I remind myself that I have an Everlasting Covenant with Jesus. I cover myself daily with His Blood and thank Him for healing. In Exodus 15:26, we are reminded that Jehovah Rapha is the Lord that heals.

Although many Christians are deceived and believe that healing is not a part of our Covenant, know that this is a lie. Some leaders are of the belief that healing ceased after the death of John, the last of the original twelve apostles. Jesus Christ, the same yesterday, today and forever reminds us that the Healer has not changed. Healing is timeless for the believer. It is a part of our Covenant. In the Early Church (that I am actively chasing its experience), the early fathers and bishops recorded the following:

> Those who are in truth His disciples, receiving grace from Him, do in His name perform miracles,,,and truly drive out devils.,,Others still heal the sick by laying their hands upon them and they are made whole. IRENAEUS, A.D. 200

> Many heathen amongst us are being healed by Christians from whatsoever sickness they have, so abundant are the miracles in our midst. Theodore of Mopsueste, A.D. 429

> In the Early Church, there were believers who received the gift of healing from God, confidently to the glory of God." CLEMENT, A.D. 275

> And some give evidence of having received through their faith a marvelous power by the cures which they perform, revoking no other name over those who need their help that of the God of all things, and of Jesus, along with a mention of His history. For these means we too have seen many persons freed from grievous calamities, and other ills, which could be cured neither by men or devils. ORIGEN, A.D. 250

Through my studies I learned that the Early Church believers were rarely sick. They laid hands on the sick and sent for the elders to continue the work of the Church. They laid hands on those outside of the faith, who became converts after witnessing and experiencing the power of healing. (James 5: 14-15)

In what many believers refer to as The Great Commission; Jesus said belevers would lay hands on the sick and they shall recover. (Mark 16:18) If He wanted anyone to be sick or if He was putting sickness on anybody, why did He provide healing in our Covenant? Our Everlasting Covenant, Redemptive Plan, Salvation and Wellness Plan are all in One and Inclusive for the believers.

Yes, in the Old Testament God allowed sickness and disease to come upon the people as punishment and judgment. (Deuteronomy 28: 15-46) In the New Testament and New Covenant, Jesus paid our penalty by taking all our sins, weaknesses, lacks, infirmities, sicknesses and diseases upon Him. "Christ hath redeemed us from the curse of the law, being made a curse for us: for it is written, Cursed is every one that hangeth on a tree". Galatians 3:13

In 2015, my mother was residing in a retirement facility in my home town. This was about three hours east of where I live. On a Sunday, I was telephoned by a nurse stating that the doctor visited my mother and could not determine the origin of her bleeding. She would be transferred to a larger hospital for testing. The hospital was one hour west of my mother. The hospital could not see her until the following Wednesday. Each day, I inquired about her condition and she was still bleeding. On that Wednesday, I traveled to the hospital to meet my mother's transport van. The hospital was ninety minutes east of my home.

I arrived thirty minutes before my mother. When she arrived, she was drowsy from a mild sedative for travel. She was scared because of the unfamiliar surroundings. I placed her wheelchair between my legs. When she waked she said, "I knew you would be here." Those words will forever ring in my heart as I hugged and comforted her.

The gynecologist could not determine the origin of the bleeding. God gave us favor and the gynecologist referred us to the hospital for treatment with the equipment to further test mother the same day. One hour later, we were at another location in that city and hundreds of images and scans were being taken. This is day four of bleeding.

Two hours later, mother was mildly sedated and placed in the transport van to return to the retirement facility. She was still bleeding and the technician stated that the doctor would be in contact with me after reading the images. On the way back home, I talked to my Father. I reminded him of the woman with the issue of blood for twelve years. I reminded him that she was healed and did not have covenant rights. I decreed and declared that my mother had a covenant with the Father which included healing. I used my prayer language (prayed in tongues) and thanked Father for my mother. I commanded the bleeding in my mother's body to stop Now in Jesus name while I was driving home. I was home in ninety minutes. I called the retirement facility as soon as I returned home. The nurse assured me that my mother was resting in her bed and the bleeding HAD STOPPED. The next morning I called and there was NO bleeding. My mother is in heaven now. She lived four years after this incident and NEVER had another bleeding incident. Speak to your problem and see it disappear.

Healing belongs to us. It was secured, provided and given to every believer as a gift. As stated in Galatians 3:13, I am redeemed of the Curse of the Law. The curses are outlined specifically in Deutcronomy 28: 15-46 and can be divided in three categories: sickness, death and poverty. Although Jesus redeemed us from sickness, death and poverty when He died for us on the Cross, it is OUR CHOICE to believe and receive Jesus' Gift. The curse is present. The curse is not dead. The curse was not removed. We were removed from the curse because we made the decision and choice to live in our Gift of Redemption. "Beloved, I wish above all things that thou mayest prosper and be in good health, even as thy soul prospereth". (III John 2)

Divine Protection

The Blessing in
the Anointing Oil

*"Is any sick among you? let him call for the elders of
the church; and let them pray over him, anointing
him with oil in the name of the Lord:"*

JAMES 5:14

To anoint means to be set apart, empowered and protected. The greek word of anoint is comprised of <u>chrio</u> (smear or rub oil) and <u>aleipho</u> (to anoint). Isaiah 10:27 describes the anointing as the burden removing and yoke destroying power of God. It is one of our weapons used against the devil. The anointing delivers God's people and set captives free. Anointing is a traditional Jewish custom to welcome visitors to their homes as a gift of hospitality. In the early church, believers anointed themselves for refreshing and healing. This form of anointing would revive and energize their bodies.

Oil was used in the Bible for medicinal purposes. The shepherds used oil for healing the sheep as they were injured in everyday activities. When I purchase anointing oil, I take time to pray over the oil. I only use the oil for empowerment and protection. This oil is not used for cooking. It is set aside for consecration purposes.

Although the oil is not a magical formula; it is a reminder of Jesus' ministry on earth. After Jesus called the twelve disciples, He sent them forth in pairs of two. Their mission was to preach, cast out devils and anoint the sick with oil for healing and according to Mark 6:13. I use the anointing oil in my personal life and ministry. During my travels, I always anoint my hotel room immediately upon arrival. Why? I do not know who and what the room was used for the night, days and weeks before I arrived. The room could have been used for adultery, premarital sex, pornography, alcohol and illicit drug abuse, anger, rage, profane conversation, etc. I use the oil to anoint the door, walls, television, bed, etc. driving all demonic spirits out and ushering in the presence of the Lord. I believe the anointing oil is a symbol of blessing and covers me like a shield.

My husband, children and I anoint our homes declaring that we are covered by the Blood of Jesus and reside in our Father's divine protection. We anoint our vehicles, homes and workplaces regularly. It is our belief that we do not have to allow demonic spirits in our space. The anointing oil symbolizes our faith in the promises of God.

Last year, an Apostolic Minister and a dear friend was hosting a Conference in my city. While leaving the parking lot, a minister approached my car asking whether I had anointing oil with me. This minister wanted to use my oil to anoint a lady who wanted her prayer language of tongues. We laid hands on this lady while applying the anointing oil and her prayer language of tongues came forth. We were in the parking lot on a major US highway, anointing, speaking in tongues and praising God. I believe in the power of the church corporate anointing.

I remember hosting a Conference in which several fivefold ministers attended. During this Conference, I was led to anoint all present. The anointing oil was poured in a large bowl in the pulpit area and had been prayed over for healing amd miracles. As each minister passed through the area, each would wash their hands in the bowl. They would shake off most of the oil in the bowl. My ministry provided a small engraved hand towel as a gift to each minister. Each person would dry their hands with their towel. No one was talking, we were worshiping God. One of the believers wanted his prayer language of tongues. As he lifted his hands from the bowl, his prayer language started flowing. A dear pastor friend from the northeastern part of our state related the following to me: The Conference was on a Saturday. She took the hand towel back to her place of worship on Sunday. The hand towel was completely dry. On Wednesday night at midweek services, the congregation started praying and she was led to use the hand towel. The towel was wet and oozing oil. Using the towel, she ministered healing to those present and healings manifested. For several weeks, the towel would ooze oil during their prayer time with healings manifesting in the gathering.

As I anoint my forehead with oil, I am activating my faith for God's protection and healing. The Hebrew word for oil is *shemen.* Jesus Christ, the Anointed One and His Anointing was presssed and crushed for me. His anointing provide me the assurance that no evil, no disease and no harm can come near me. "Touch not mine anointed, and do my prophets no harm." Psalm 105:15 As believers, we are the anointed ministers of Jesus Christ. Jesus paid my price.

My prayer over my anointing oil is in the name of the Father, the Son, Jesus Christ and by the power of Holy Spirit. I decree that the oil is set apart as my Holy Anointing Oil with power to cast out demons and to heal the sick according to the Word in Mark 16: 13 and James 5: 14-15. I declare that this oil sets me apart unto my Father and makes me more than a conqueror and overcomer. The oil honors my Father and man and brings glory to Jesus Christ. This anointing oil gives me gladness, victory and empowers me for service and ministry unto Father. This anointing oil speaks of the finished work of Jesus Christ and provides me protection from evil. This anointing oil blesses me and gives me complete victory and prosperity in Jesus Christ.

I remember in Ruth 3:3; Naomi (Ruth's mother in law) instructed her to anoint herself before meeting Boaz. This directive by Naomi resulted in holy matrimony and a place in the genealogy of Jesus. This gives me assurance and permission of anointing myself in the name of the Father, Son and Holy Spirit. Anointing myself symbolizes the gift of Holy Spirit residing in me, Who empowers me to succeed in Jesus Name!

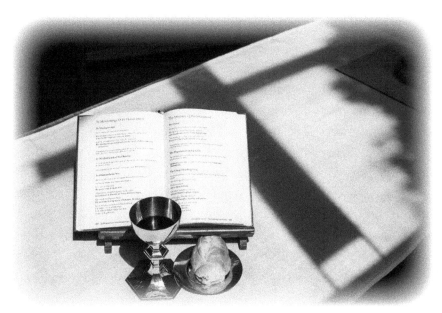

The Healing Meal

My Favorite Meal

---◆---

"And they continually daily with one accord in the temple, and breaking bread from house to house, did eat their meat with gladness and singleness of heart".

ACTS 3:46

I am eternally grateful for Jesus sacrifice on the Cross for me. I learned decades ago what the Lord's Supper meant to the Early Church. The first century believers received Holy Communion from house to house everyday. They had a relationship with Jesus which afforded them the opportunity to receive the power of the meal. They were aware of the redemptive work of Christ and had faith in His finished work.

Koinonia is the original Greek word for communion. It means fellowship and denotes intimate participation. Partaking in the Holy Communion or Lord's Supper should be an intimate time between the Lord and us. During this time we should block out everything and come into His presence with love and thanksgiving,

When I was a child and a member of a traditional denominational church, I was taught the following: (1) Only the pastor can minister the Lord's Supper; (2) Women can not serve it, however they prepare the elements; (3) Do not participate if you have sinned or have negative thoughts and (4) if you spill the grape juice during the preparation, someone in the fellowship will die within thirty days. HOW IGNORANT!

None of the above is true.

Every believer can minister (serve) the Lord's Supper. I receive the Lord's Supper often and I serve myself. I view myself receiving the Lord's Supper from Jesus with the knowledge that He loves me. I receive knowing that this sacred meal is possible because of what Jesus did for me. I am so excited that I can receive the Lord's Supper whenever I want to. I am a fivefold ministry teacher. I am not a pastor. If error #1 was true, I could only receive the Lord's Supper when I am at the meeting place and the pastor decides to serve. There are some church memberships who receive the meal once a year; others three times yearly; others monthly and a few weekly.

I would not be able to minister the Lord's Supper alone in my house if Error #2 was true. I would need a male pastor, however error #2 above is wrong teaching also. My daughters are female. They are lay ministers and they serve themselves the Lord's Supper as often as they desire the meal. The meal can be ministered by any Christian.

Error #3 comes from wrong interpretation of 1 Corinthians 11:27 -30 "Wherefore whosoever shall eat this bread, and drink this cup of the Lord, unworthily, shall be guilty of the body and blood of the Lord. But let a man examine himself, and so let him eat of that bread, and drink of that cup. For he that eateth and drinketh unworthily, eateth and drinketh damnation to himself, not discerning the Lord's body. For this cause many are weak and sickly among you, and many sleep". Wrong teaching said we are unworthy and unqualified. The correct interpretation has NOTHING to do with our deeds; it has EVERYTHING to do with the MANNER in which we receive the Lord's Supper. Know why we are partaking. Know what the elements represent. Know why we are remembering the Lord's death. Receive this meal in remembrance of Jesus' love and sacrifice by reminding oneself of Jesus scourging, beatings, hanging naked, mockery and humiliation directed toward him, three hours of darkness, divine exchange of His Righteousness for our sins, the veil being torn giving the believer access to our Heavenly Father and the His death. All of this was done in LOVE.

Error #4 has nothing to do with whether we spill the juice or wine in preparng the elements. Praise God that Jesus' Blood was spilled for us.

What elements are used in the Lord's Supper? The bread and wine are used. The bread is symbolic of Jesus' body and healing. Jesus is the Bread of Life. (John 6:35) When the Syrophenician woman asked Jesus to heal her demon possessed daughter, Jesus responded that He could not give her the children's bread. He was using bread interchangeably with healing. She did not ask for food to eat. She wanted healing. This passage is recorded in Matthew 15: 21-28.

When I receive the Bread, I am receiving Jesus' body into my body. I am receiving perfect health. I am reminding myself of 1 John 4:17; as Jesus is, so am I. Is Jesus sick, weak or lacking in Heaven? NO, therefore I am well, strong and divine health belongs to me. As I receive the Bread, I remember that Jesus' body was brutually beaten and repeatedly struck. From His arrest in the Garden of Gethsemane to Golgotha (Calvary and Place of the Skull), he was spat upon, mocked, humiliated, beaten and scourged so that my body can be healed and whole.

"Lord Jesus thank You for taking my sickness, disease, infirmity and weakness to the Cross. When the lashes fell on Your back at the whipping and scorging posts, this condition in my body was destroyed, therefore you are a trespasser. You do not have a right to linger in my body. (I speak the condition and say)_____, get out of my body. By the stripes of Jesus, I was healed, therefore I am healed. Healing, restoration and creative miracles appear now in Jesus' Name". Thank You Jesus!

When I receive His Blood, I am receiving His SINLESS BLOOD that was shed for me. Without the shedding of blood, there is NO remission of sins. "For I will be merciful to their unrighteousness, and their sins and their lawless deeds I will remember np more." (Hebrews 8:12) In the past, God remembered our sins and punished to the third and fourth generations as recorded in Exodus 20:5. In our New Covenant, God says "No More" meaning that He will never again remember our sins. He will not count our sins against us. God punished all of our sins in the body of His Son, Jesus. In receiving His Blood, I am thankful that I have been forgiven of my past, present and future sins. I remind myself that there is NOTHING in my bloodline that can deny me the GIFT of FORGIVENESS. Thank You Jesus!

When we partake of the Lord's body, there is an infusion of His incorruptible life into our bodies. Leviticus 17:11 declares the life of the flesh is in the blood. When blood is separatd from flesh, death comes. On the Cross, Jesus' blood was separated from His flesh causing death. In the Lord's Supper, Jesus' blood and flesh are reunited which brings forth life. Adam introduced sickness and death to the world by eating in the Garden of Eden. Jesus brought health and life back to us by eating the Lord's Supper.

As I receive the blood in the cup, I remember that Jesus shed His blood for me. "Jesus, thank You for your shed blood that has washed away my sins and made me righteous. I am the Righteousness of God in Jesus Christ. I am forgiven of all past, present and future sins in Jesus' Name". Thank You Jesus!

I urge you to do as the Early Church practiced eating and drinking this meal often. Study the meaning and do not allow the Lord's Supper to become a ritual. Remember this is the BODY of JESUS CHRIST. Receive the meal in love, thanksgiving and appreciation of the One Who made the sacrifice and paid the price, JESUS CHRIST.

Restoration of Fivefold Ministry

Restoration of Fivefold Ministry

"And he gave some, apostles; and some, prophets; and some, evangelists; and some, pators and teachers; for the perfecting of the saints, for the work of the ministry, for the edifying of the body of Christ: till we all come in the unity of the faith, and of the knowledge of the Son of God, unto a perfect man, unto the measure of the stature of the fulness of Christ: that we henceforth be no more children, tossed to and fro, and carried about with every wind of doctrine, by the sleight of men, and cunning craftiness, whereby they lie in wait to deceive; but speaking thetruth in love, may grow up into him in all things, which is the head, even Christ: from whom the whole body fitly joined together and compacted b that which every joint supplieth, according to the effectual working in the measure of every part, maketh incease of the body unto the edifying of itself in love".

EPHESIANS 4: 11-16

Every born again believer is a preacher. Preaching what? When Saul was persecuting the church, the believers were scattered and fled Jerusalem. The apostles remained in Jerusalem. The believers who fled preached the word (Jesus) everywhere they went. (Acts 8: 1-4) My personal definition for minister is a born again believer rendering service to God, the church and the world by active and continuous practice of a Christian lifestyle. The word minister is servant and the word ministry is service. Are you a servant and where do you render your service?

Acts 6: 1-7 speaks of Christians being ordained to do the work of the ministry. These people are Christian leaders (lay ministers); not fivefold ministers. Lay ministers are equally important to the church as fivefold ministers. All fivefold ministers begin as lay ministers. When God calls a lay minister to a fivefold ministry office, he or she is given a greater responsibility in the Body of Christ.

Fivefold ministers are Pulpit Ministers. Lay Ministers serve mankind in their careers, positions and secular employment. Christians minister in the fields of education, law, medicine, retail, sales, engineering, business, community service and other vocations. By glorifying God in all we do; our ministry is done unto the Lord. (Colossians 3:17)

My present assignment to the Church is the Restoration of Fivefold Ministry. Who are the fivefold ministers? They are Apostles, Prophets, Evangelists, Pastors and Teachers as recorded in Ephesians 4:11. Who placed these leaders in the Church? <u>JESUS</u> God placed the anointing of specific gifts and the grace to use the gifts in the Body of Christ. God's intent is that these ministers be received as Gifts in the Body of Christ. In Romans 11:13, Paul referred to these Gifts as Offices. These ministers should be full time service personnel and financially compensated. These mnisters are called to work together as ONE UNIT. The office of pastor was NEVER to lead the Church alone. The fivefold ministry office of pastor is only One Fifth of the Leadership Team ordained by Jesus to lead the church. Each fivefold minister has a Special Anointing and Grace to fulfill the Call of Church Leadership and Government.

It is impossible for one person or office to effectively lead the church. As a team, unit or group the fivefold ministers work together and can do the work effectively as Jesus organized the church. Jesus is the Head of the Church and is the Only One Who can say how the church should be governed. (1 Corinthians 11:13) In Matthew 16:18 when the Holy Spirit revealed to Peter the true identity of Jesus;

He built His Church based on Himself (the Truth) as recorded in Matthew 16:18. We, the Church, obey the Head, Who revealed to Paul that the church is to be governed by Fivefold Ministers.

What are the responsibilites of the fivefold ministers? The Apostle is the "Sent One" in the Body of Christ and sets in order the Mission of the Church. Apostles are commissioned by God to plant churches in areas that need a gathering place for believers. After praying all night, Jesus chose twelve from the larger number of disciples and appointed them as Apostles. (Luke 6:13) Paul became an Apostle in which he affirmed his calling in his Early Church Writings.

Prophets bring supernatural revelation and insight to the seasons that the Church is experiencing by sharing Godly wisdom. Prophets are commissioned by God for deep revelation in the signs of the times and future events. They have a special anointing of hearing God's voice. Prophets give warnings to the church in order to change behavior and alter destructive and devastating behavior as recorded in Acts 21: 10-13.

Evangelists have a hunger for souls to be saved and seek opportunities to share the Gospel with everyone. Evangelists are commissioned by God with a supernatural gift and special anointing to bring people to the Lord. In my forty plus years of active ministry, I have witnessed two types of evangelists: Itinerant and Marketplace. The Itinerant Evangelist is a fivefold minister who usually ministers from a pulpit or platform. They are invited by congregations to preach revivals and camp meetings to stir up a refreshing to the Body of Christ. (11 Timothy 4:5) Marketplace Evangelists minister publicly and privately in small groups or one on one. They do not operate on schedules. They recognize a need and minister through the compassion of Jesus and their service anointing. (Acts 21:8) Today, we see them ministering on store aisles.

Pastors nurture the Body of Christ by demonstrating the love of Jesus Christ and counseling the sheep. Pastors are commissioned by God to shepherd the spiritual needs of the people. They have a special anointing of guiding people from brokenness to wholeness. Pastors and Bishops have the same qualifications as recorded in 1 Timothy

3: 1-7. This is the fivefold minister that God calls according to His heart which shall feed you with knowledge and understanding as recorded in Jeremiah 3:15.

Teachers teach and dissect the Word of God with wisdom, truth and simplicity. Teachers are commissioned by God to the Study of the Word. Teachers instruct and expound on the text, customs, traditions and meanings in reference to the present time frame. Teachers have a special anointing for explaining the Word while exposing lies, confusion and misinformation. The teachings of the fivefold minister is judged more harshly than the others as recorded in James 3:1.

The purpose of the Fivefold Ministers is the developing and perfecting work of the ministry and edification of the Church. Fivefold ministers are assigned to equip the saints to do the work of the ministry. Fivefold ministers begin the process of maturation by teaching and demonstrating Christian lifestyles. Through lay ministers, the Body of Christ is edified (built up) and matured. Perfecting in Ephesians 4:12 means gamar which is fully preparing the Church for the work of the ministry. This can ONLY happen if the five offices (GIFTS) work together as One Unit.

Is Fivefold Ministry still relevant today? Yes, God ordained these ministers to serve until the WHOLE BODY of CHRIST (the Church) becomes mature and fully developed in the unity of the faith and knowledge of Jesus as stated in Ephesians 4:13. Church fellowships contact Moore Life Institute (the 501 (c) 3 nonprofit christian ministry that I oversee as founder, facilitator and executive director) for assistance in minister ordinations. MLI offers several courses and workshops to train ministers (lay and fivefold) for effective service in the Body of Christ. After completion of these classes, those local fellowships ordain the ministers.

Children fluctuate and are easily deceived. Tossed to and from like a wave in the sea with every fad captivating the attention and actions of immature Christians (facebook, twitter, instagram, cell phone, change of service contemporary, tradition, worship, no Sunday Morning Sunday School/Discipleship Training - Bible Study, etc.) Sleight meaning gambling with deception of immature Christians as the sleight of hand in a card game skilled in cunning and trickery to deceive as stated in Ephesians 4:14.

Ephesians 4:15 ministers' behavior must show love. Fivefold ministers are not to beat listeners with their beliefs. They are to feed the sheep and the sheep should demonstrate love, not sarcasm, arrogance and ridicule in speech and behavior. Ministers must teach and preach the Truth instructed by the Head of the Church.

Just as every part of our physical anatomy has its individual function to be ONE PERFECT WHOLE BODY, the Body of Christ (each minister) should function to serve the Lord Jesus Christ, Who is our Head. (Ephesians 1: 22-23) Unity among believers is important because it takes a collective effort for the Church to work (minister) as ONE.

Why is the Fivefold Ministry inactive in majority of the Church Fellowships today? As Healing, Faith and Grace were restored to the church after its presence seldom manifested, fivefold ministry has to be restored. Healing Evangelists preached healing and the manifestation came forth. Faith was taught and the Church embraced the teaching and witnessed supernatural results. Grace was restored and believers learned that we were no longer under the Law. Finally, we know who we are because of unmerited favor, living in Grace and experiencing amazing breakthroughs.

Believers, please join us in the restoration of Fivefold Ministry to the Church. Why? This is the formula that Jesus set for the Church to equip and mature the believer. The Church will never be what Jesus created this living organism to be until we follow His directive. Jesus' mandate for the Church must continue until all believes are mature, come into the unity of faith and fitly joined together. We, the Church, have not achieved the intent or goal of Ephesians 4: 11-16.

Eyes of church leaders are being spiritually open to the biblical truth about fivefold ministry. It was never the intent of God that pastors lead congregations alone. Pastors are only one fifth of the Leadership Team; however they govern alone and are financially compensated alone. Each of the fivefold ministers has value and a special anointing and grace given by God to govern the Body of Christ as a team.

The early church followed God's structure for the local congregations. The leaders were fivefold ministers referred to as elders and overseers. Refer to Acts 14:23 and Acts 20:28 "Take heed therefore unto yourselves and to all the flock, over the which the Holy Ghost hath made you OVERSEERS, to feed the church of God, which he hath purchased with his own blood."

Through ignorance and error, the office of pastor was elevated to a position of rulership single handedly. How did thia happen? Church history states in the First Century, the Catholic Church consented to one person as the Patriarch of the Catholic Church and called him the POPE. Later, the local fellowship (Parish) elevated single leadership to a male elder. bishop or priest.

According to church history, the non Catholic believers changed their local fellowships government from plurality (fivefold ministry) to single male rulership. This happened after the death of the original Early Church Apostles, who followed the mandate of Jesus. According to Bible scholars Ignatius of Antioch, a disciple of Apostle John and a second generation church leader, started teaching and writing to the Early Church about changing the leadership. He advocated for single church hierarchy. He objected to a group of overseers (fivefold ministers) working as a single unit to one male being the solo leader. The person was called Bishop and is now referred to as pastor or bishop. The other leaders (Apostle, Prophet, Evangelist and Teacher) were ranked under the pastor in authority and position. Ignatius of Antioch argued that the new church structure would prevent church splits and preserve correct beliefs. He taught that one must view the bishop/pastor as the Lord Himself. The above is recorded in Early Church Writings - Lightfoot, 88.

I argue the following for Fivefold Ministry Restoration: It is Jesus' mandate for Church Leadership and Government. It is a protective structure that ensures Accountability. In Fivefold Ministry Leadership, should a leader go wayward or teaches in error, correction is available from the other leaders. (Acts 20:30) Fivefold ministry in the local assembly protects against the danger of one person gaining an exalted position. In 3 John 9, Diotrephes, not called or ordained by

God, placed himself in a church leadership position and encouraged thc Church to stop supporting Apostle John, which action caused a church split.

Fivefold ministers are not dictators. They do not make all the decisions of the local assembly. (Matthew 18: 15-18 and 1 Corinthians 14:26) The local assembly takes part in the decision making process. Although the term"Fivefold" is not mentioned in the Bible, Paul teaches the plurality of church leadership mandated by Jesus in detail in Ephesians 4: 11-16 and 1 Corinthians 12: 28-31. Five comes from the number of offices and gifts in the Body of Christ. The terms Trinity and Rapture are no found in most Bibles, however Christians believe these truths. Trinity refers to God, the Son and Holy Spirit as One. Rapture refers to the catching away of the church.

The error and ignorance of the second generation church leaders led to the dilemna that the church is suffering today. In the Early Church, male and female ministers were common; however the church changes in the second generation creating male ministry dominance. There are denominations {I do not believe in denominations. They are devisive and not biblical.) who do not accept females in church leadership. Today, people who are called to pulpit ministry, because of ignorance and error, think there is only one ministry office. This error leads to service in the office of pastor. Why? They have not studied the Word for themselves with the help of Holy Spirit and/or listened to error from the pulpit pastor. Believers who do not search the scripture led by Holy Spirit accept, promote and support ministers in the wrong position. They know that the pastor is usually the only fivefold minister receiving a regular salary. The other four fivefold ministers usually receive financial compensation when contacted by the pastor or local assembly to fill in or conduct a special service. Usually this financial compensation is meager compared to the pastor's salary. On the average, the non pastor ministers receive financial compensation a few times during the year which require employment in secular positions to pay their bills.

I have taught fivefold ministry workshops for years. These workshops are offered to fellowships and ministries in which I am the facilitator and teach in detail fivefold ministry. A male pastor of a congregation of approximately 100 people heard the teaching from one of my fivefold ministry workshops. He was convicted concerning his calling. He knew that he was called to pulpit ministry, but now questioned what position or office. He remarked that he identified more with an evangelist than a pastor. Because of teaching error, he was taught that his calling was pastor. Why? No other options were discussed. Ephesians 4:11-16 was ignored. He stated that he was sure now that his calling was evangelist. What was he going to do? He remarked that he was in debt and needed the weekly pastoral salary to maintain his lifestyle. He further stated that he would remain silent until he is out of debt; then resign and continue in ministry as an evangelist. It is sad that this man is willing to continue in a lie for many years because of his pride and financial benefits. It is not my assignment to reveal his identity. It is my assignment to fulfill my calling of Restoring Fivefold Ministry to the Body of Christ.

I experienced a similar dilemna in my calling. I have been approached a few times about pastoring. Each time, I explain that I am one of the fivefold ministers; but not in the office of pastor. My gift, calling and office is teacher. Although I have worked with pastors very well, my contribution was from a teacher/bible scholar perspective. My calling is not pastoral dominant. Although I am a member of a local fellowship, I preach and teach often at different ministries. It is only when I am invited to other ministries, that I am financially compensated for my gift. I was offered a pastoral position last year with several benefits (large weekly salary; local domicile; retirement plan; medical benefits; vacation pay, etc.). Was I tempted? NO!!! I love my calling. I know the worth of each fivefold ministry office to the Body of Christ. The teacher is needed. I will not vacate my calling for material benefits. I do understand the temptations that others surrender to for the fame, pride and material benefits; however I value my spiritual calling above physical desires.

Some fivefold ministers change offices being directed by God while others change offices due to pride and material benefits. I am asked the following question often: What is the most important fivefold ministry office? My answer is always the same. The offices are equal. Whatever office you are in need of at the time, is the most important. Let me clarify. I have each of these ministry offices in my life. I financially support each office on a regular basis. When I need a prophet, that office is the most important to me at that time. I approach each office in the same manner with the utmost respect and appreciation. Fivefold ministers who change offices for personal interests are of the opinion that one office elevates their status above the other. There has been an influx of fivefold ministers moving to the office of apostle. Whoa! Whoa! Some of these ministers' spiritual attributes changed which placed them in another office; however others are being deceived. In the early church, Titus and Timothy were called to be pastors, embraced the calling, grew and remained in their calling. Church leaders, please be careful. If the current pattern continues, the role of pastor as the solo ruler of the church (which is error) will be changed to apostle as the single ruler (another error). Jesus gave us the plan: fivefold ministry as church government.

I want to address the believer who loves the game of basketball. I am a former college basketball player who loves and enjoys the game, collegiate and professional. There are five positions in basketball: point guard, shooting guard, small forward, power forward and center. I played the position of point guard. The point guard is the General and must see the floor. The point guard must know where the other players are to make sure that the ball is successfully passed. The point guard usually start the offensive cycle for the team. I can not play by myself. I can not take the ball out of bound; throw it to myself in bound, dribble 24 seconds while being chased by five people from the opposing team; shoot the ball and grabbing the rebound. Winning is impossible without the gifts, skills and talents of the other four players. Pastors (point guards) pass the ball; stop being the lone shooter; get out of the paint; guard a player before the team (the congregation) replaces you. Pastors, the day of the Lone Ranger is over. Fivefold ministry is the Only team mandated by Jesus to function as one unit.

Churches, who do not have these ministers in their local

congregations, but want to help in the restoration of fivefold ministry are doing the following: They are opening their pulpits to fivefold ministry workshops on a regular basis. After accepting the truth of the Word; they are inviting one of the other fivefold ministers to their local assembly to preach on Sunday mornings quarterly. Pastors are respecting the apostle, prophet, evangelist and teacher as equals and financially compensating them for their gift. The goal is to have each assembly/congregation leadership team to be comprised of each fivefold minister working together as a single unit. Each minister is financially compensated and valued for the gift that is shared in the Body of Christ. Hallelujah!

Chasing the Promised Dream

Trotting into a Full Sprint

---◆---

"For we are his workmanship, created in Christ Jesus unto good works, which God hath before ordained that we should walk in them."

EPHESIANS 2:10

Thank you Church for allowing me to share and vent through these pages. You have heard my compassion and heart's cry to live end enjoy the Early Church experience. It is my intent to whet your appetite to join me in this quest. Can you remember where we were in our spiritual development before the Healing, Faith and Grace Teachings were restored to the church? We were sick, doubting and trying to receive by our works. Now, we are well, speaking the Word with manifestations and receiving our unmerited favor. We know that this life is not about what we can do, but about what JESUS HAS DONE.

Yes, we are our Father's masterpiece and created in the image of Jesus Christ. I love how the Message Bible describes our blessed condition, "Now God has us where he wants us, with all the time in this world and the next to shower grace and kindness upon us in Christ Jesus. Saving is all his idea, and all his work. All we do is trust him enough to let him do it. It's God's gift from start to finish!

We don't play the major role. If we did, we'd probably go around bragging that we'd done the whole thing! No, we neither make nor save ourselves. God does both the making and saving, He creates each of us by Christ Jesus to join him in the work he does, the good work he has gotten ready for us to do, work he had better be doing." Ephesians 2:10

If you have never accepted Jesus as your Savior and want to spend eternity with Him, pray the following: "Jesus, thank you for loving and choosing me as family. I believe that you are the Son of God, lived as man and God, was crucified on the Cross, died, was buried and raised from the dead after three days and are sitting on the right hand of God in Heaven making intercession for me now. I receive you as my Lord and Savior. Because of your finished work, I am your child and will spend eternity with you. My heart is filled with your love, peace and joy. I am the Righteousness of God in Jesus Christ."

Since we can not do anything without the assistance of the Holy Spirit working through us, why not do everything Jesus way? When we do life Jesus way, we succeed. Jesus' way was demonstrated in the success of the Early Church. The believers studied, practiced and lived the Word. They prayed the Word in the natural and prayed in Tongues in the Spirit. The result was supernatural living and being. The early church knew the power of praise and worship and made it a part of their daily existence. The First Century believers walked in divine health. They were not sick. They practiced healing the sick by speaking the Word and laying on hands. These Christians truly believed the Word. Signs, wonders and miracles were active in their ministries. They gave ALL the CREDIT to Jesus with prayers for boldness to spread the Salvation Package to all. They remembered who and what they were before meeting Jesus. They knew that they were sinking sand before Jesus and now solid rocks after receiving Jesus as their Savior. The Early Church believed in the power of the anointing oil. When smeared or rubbed on, the anointing oil becomes the burden removing and yoke destroying power needed in our lifestyles. First Century Christians knew the power of the Body of Jesus and the Blood of Jesus. They received the Lord's Supper from house to house. The power of the Lord's Supper kept them physically and mentally strong to do the work of the ministry. In order to successfully live the life that Jesus died for them to have, they approached the ministry as one unit. The Early Church embraced the spirit of togetherness and unity by living the fivefold ministry lifestyle. Jesus Christ is the Head of the Church and the first century believers (Christians) did ministry the only way - His Way. At one time, the believers were referred to as the Way.

This is the time for us to unite as one. We are the Church and we have been existing, not living. Jesus died for us to live the abundant life. We are the head and not the tail. We are above ONLY and not beneath. We are not in charge. We are stewards of the Creator of the Church. Join the Early Church Revolution by practicing the formula of the first century believers and reaping all the benefits of our salvation. It is my prayer that I will meet you on this journey. I truly love all of you. You are my co-laborers in ministry, regardless of ethnicity, gender, lay or fivefold minister.

Contact Information

Katherine Moore Davis, Ed.D.
Moore Life Institute
Post Office Box 6433
Bossier City, Louisiana 71171-6433
kmoorelife@aol.com

*Moore Life Institute Workshops are held at mutual and convenient sites for your audience. Dr. Katherine is the facilitator for numerous workshops developed with the aid of Holy Spirit. They will enlighten and enhance your congregation's biblical knowledge, regardless of membership size. Use the above contact information for scheduling purposes.

Lightning Source UK Ltd.
Milton Keynes UK
UKHW012121061120
372956UK00008B/438/J